Payal Dhar has been making up stories all her life. Sometimes she has got into trouble for them, but sometimes they have been published as novels and short stories, mostly for young people. She's also a freelance editor and writer, and writes on computers, technology, books, reading, games, travel and anything else that catches her interest. When nobody's looking, she either has her nose in a book, is surfing the Internet, or battling evil in a computer game.

Visit Writeside.net to find out more about Payal's work and play.

Payal Dhar

For SM and those cricket-filled days

Published by
Rupa Publications India Pvt. Ltd 2018
7/16, Ansari Road, Daryaganj
New Delhi 110002

Sales centres:
Allahabad Bengaluru Chennai
Hyderabad Jaipur Kathmandu
Kolkata Mumbai

Copyright © Payal Dhar 2018

This is a work of fiction. Names, characters, places and incidents are either the product of the author's imagination or are used fictitiously and any resemblance to any actual person, living or dead, events or locales is entirely coincidental.

All rights reserved.
No part of this publication may be reproduced, transmitted, or stored in a retrieval system, in any form or by any means, electronic, mechanical, photocopying, recording or otherwise, without the prior permission of the publisher.

ISBN: 978-81-291-4962-6

First impression 2018

10 9 8 7 6 5 4 3 2 1

The moral right of the author has been asserted.

Printed at Thomson Press India Ltd., Faridabad

This book is sold subject to the condition that it shall not, by way of trade or otherwise, be lent, resold, hired out, or otherwise circulated, without the publisher's prior consent, in any form of binding or cover other than that in which it is published.

Chapter 1

Laila heaved the canvas knapsack over the gate and then stood with her hands on her hips, trying to decide the best way over it. There were thick bars perpendicular to the ground, separated by thinner metallic circles. She put her foot on one of the circles and tested it to see if it would take her weight. It did and within seconds Laila was up and over the top of the gate, jumping down to the ground. She picked up her bag and looked around.

For many years now, she had been pushing past the bent and rickety old gate—very different from the shiny new one she'd just climbed over—and slipping into the grounds of Old Mister Marshall's long-abandoned house. The big old house itself was locked up, but it had extensive (and exciting gardens), including some ruins at the back and a pond. During her explorations, Laila had found an almost intact room amidst the ruins, with a stone ledge, which worked wonderfully as a hideout. She had secreted away a stash of sweets and biscuits in an old plastic container under the ledge, and even had a rolled-up durrie that she would lie on and read or play games on her phone. On cold winter days, she would sit up and soak in the sun filtering in through the trees. On hotter days, she would hunker down in the shade. And when it rained, the parapet was wide enough to keep her dry—mostly.

Her den at Old Mister Marshall's house was a secret. Not even her best friend Shalini knew about it and they had been friends since they were four. But now she was gone, so what did it matter?

Everything was changing, Laila thought. And not for the better. What was she going to do without Shalini? (And then there was the whole cricket scandal—but Laila had vowed not to think of that.)

To be fair, the new gate should have been an indication that things were afoot at the old house, but the cloud of gloom that hovered over Laila's head obscured her deductive powers. Her mood wasn't the only dark cloud in the vicinity. It was an overcast morning, with rain more or less certain. Plus, the summer holidays loomed large and lonely before her, and she hadn't been in a mood to let matters like a padlocked gate and a bit of rain get in her way.

The caretaker's cottage by the gate looked a little livelier than usual, with curtains in the windows, which should have been the second clue. Not to mention a clothes line with a sheet flapping on it. But Laila ignored everything and dived into the overgrown path that would take her to the back of the house.

And then, all hell broke loose.

First, there was a yell. *'Aay! Kaun hai?'*

Next, an elderly gent in a yellow T-shirt and camouflage combat pants came thundering out from between the trees. He had a stout stick nearly as long as Laila, which he thumped on the ground. *'Kaun hai?'* he shouted again, though he could see very well who it was.

Laila was so startled, she couldn't move. Till the old man picked up his stick threateningly and lumbered towards her.

She turned and fled. There was no way she would make it to the gate and climb over in time, so she tore through the overgrown bushes along the boundary wall. She knew of a hole just around the corner, slightly inconvenient but big enough to squeeze through. She threw herself through it, scrambled to her feet and ran as fast as her legs could carry her. To add insult to injury, rain started to pelt down.

That evening, pretending that her shoulder wasn't in agony from having fallen awkwardly during her escape, she overheard her parents talking about Old Mister Marshall's house having been bought by new owners, who would be moving in soon.

Great, so now her secret hideout was gone too. It was time to call the summer holidays a bust.

●

Laila's foot came away from the shallow ditch with a reluctant squelch. Disgusted, she shook her leg. Globs of mud flew everywhere. There was an awful smell, of rotten things and stinky earth. She groaned at the sight of her shoes and the bottom two inches of her (almost new) jeans.

When she had gone back to Old Mister Marshall's house the day after her unceremonious retreat, the gates had been wide open, and a team of gardeners had been trimming the lawn. Trucks carrying construction material were dumping sand, cement and other stuff. Workers were going in and out of the old house, whose doors had been thrown open too. The crotchety old guard had been around as well. Poor Laila hadn't even got a chance to rescue her stuff.

After that, every single day of the summer holidays, she had taken the shortcut down the hill towards the lane leading to the old house to see what was going on. The overgrown lawns had been trimmed, the flowerbeds weeded and cleaned, the house itself painted, polished and repaired.

On the day that Laila stumbled into the mud-filled pothole by the side of the road, a humungous container truck was parked at the mouth of the lane, effectively blocking any traffic in and out of the colony. Its rear end lay open, and large, shadowy shapes were visible inside. A convoy of uniformed men struggled with heavy pieces of furniture down the ramp from the truck and on to a trolley-like thing with wheels, which they pulled towards the house.

Laila wondered if the new owners of the house had any kids and if so, whether she could make friends with them. She'd heard rumours of an indoor swimming pool.

She walked casually up to the gates and watched with interest as something that might have been a piano was manhandled into the house.

The boundary wall had been painted anew as well and there was a new name plate that said 'SJ House'. The house had originally been called Flycatcher Mansion and it had lain empty for decades—at least as far as Laila knew—because it was rumoured to be cursed. Old Mr Marshall was said to have scoffed at superstition, but then his business *had* gone bankrupt and his wife and children *had* died in an accident. That hadn't stopped him from living there, though, alone and lonely, it was said. Some people also said the house was haunted, but Laila didn't believe in ghosts.

A group of four or five men came out from the house. They stopped for a rest by the gate, swigging from water bottles. It was a pleasant, cool day, but they were drenched in sweat.

'Who are the new owners?' Laila called to them in Hindi.

One of them, mopping the top of his bald head with a towel, shook his head. 'Don't know.'

The front doors were wide open and even though the hall was littered with packing material, it was clear that things had been dusted, polished, repaired and repainted inside. The marble steps and the pillars were shining, so were the huge double doors with their ornate knockers. On the first floor, somebody was hanging curtains, and one of the top-floor windows framed a carpenter busy sawing something. There were solar heaters on the roof—Laila had watched them being installed.

There was some commotion at the end of the lane. The movers put away their bottles and got up. The lorry seemed to be rearranging itself and a sleek silver car squeezed its way past it and came towards them. The windows were rolled up and darkened.

The car drove past Laila, into the gates and up the driveway, pulling up in front of the house. The driver jumped out and rushed to open the rear door. A woman, probably older than Laila's parents, dressed in jeans and a billowy white shirt, with sunglasses pushed up on top of her head, got out. She had a large handbag.

She could see heads emerging from the other side too, including one tall man wearing a hat, but she couldn't see his face. There was a third person, someone smaller, but the car blocked Laila's view. Everyone went inside, while the driver went around to open the boot. Phoolchand, the caretaker, and his son came out to help him haul out suitcases and bags.

Laila watched for a while, wondering if she had the guts to go up to them and say hello. Part of her wanted to do it to spite Phoolchand too. So she took off down the driveway, but by the time she got to the front door, the family or whoever they were, were well indoors. Only the driver remained and as she approached, Phoolchand reappeared.

'What do you want?' he demanded.

'I have a message for the family,' said Laila boldly.

'What message?'

'It's for them.'

'They're tired and resting,' said Phoolchand shortly. 'You will have to tell me.'

Laila crossed her arms. 'Then I will come back later.'

'As you wish.' He picked up a bag and went back inside.

Bah, that went well, Laila thought. She looked up and as if on cue, a curtain twitched on the first floor and a face appeared behind the glass pane of one of the windows. It stared at her.

'Who's that?' Laila asked the driver as the face disappeared from the window.

'Baby,' said the driver helpfully.

'Baby? She didn't look like a baby.'

'Not a baby. Madam's daughter and Bhaiya's sister.'

That wasn't any more helpful. 'But what's her name?'

'I don't know. I only joined work today.'

Chapter 2

'Meet me at the gate tomorrow at nine,' Shalini told Laila over the phone that evening. 'There's something I want to show you.'

'What?'

'It's a surprise.'

Fortunately, the school that Laila went to had a hostel, which meant that Shalini could continue studying there even though she no longer lived in the town. In fact, Shalini had always been a boarder at Rosebud Academy. The reason was that her parents were constantly travelling—her father was an airline pilot and her mother an archaeologist. During the holidays, Shalini stayed with an elderly aunt, not far from Laila's house, and one of her parents would try to come down for a visit.

Laila had never been able to understand what it was like for her to rarely meet her parents. But Shalini had seemed happy—even though her aunt was a bit of an overprotective stick-in-the-mud—so she rarely dwelt on it. Sometime last year, however, Shalini's father decided to quit flying planes and started a business, and her mother decided to stop digging up old sites and switch to teaching. Unfortunately, they decided to do all of that in a city two thousand kilometres away. At least they didn't think they needed to change her school.

So the next morning, a Saturday, saw Laila at Rosebud Academy bright and early. Shalini was already standing by the gate and the two girls screeched when they saw each other.

'Shalini!'

'Laila!'

Om Prakash, the guard, who was sitting on a stool outside his little room by the gates of the school, sunning himself and reading one of those luridly covered Hindi novels that he seemed to have a never-ending supply of, jumped up in alarm. His book fell to the ground and snapped shut.

'*Baap re*,' he said, a hand on his chest. 'You girls will give me a heart attack!' He bent to retrieve his book. 'Now look, I've lost my page.' He flapped the book at them, pretending to be angry, 'Get away now!'

They ran off, laughing.

'So, how are you?' Shalini asked.

'Bored,' replied Laila. 'And you? How's it in the big city?'

Shalini's face clouded over. 'It's big and you don't know anyone and you can't go out anywhere by yourself. I'm so glad to be back at school.' She linked arms with Laila and looked up in surprise like she was noticing her friend for the first time. 'Hey, you've grown taller—you're taller than me now!'

'Er, sorry?' Laila said. Vertical was the only direction she had been growing lately. Unlike Shalini. 'You've grown too—though not taller.'

Shalini didn't say anything, but didn't look too displeased. They walked towards the school building, arm in arm.

'You'll never guess what's happening,' Laila said. 'Remember Old Mister Marshall's house?'

'The haunted place?'

'It was not haunted! But yeah, that one. It's been sold and renovated, and someone's moved in.'

Shalini's mouth fell open. 'No way! That house was cursed.'

'You really believe all that nonsense?'

'Who bought it?'
'I don't know. But it looks quite fancy now.'
'Wow, I bet. What are the new people like?'
'I don't know. They seem to keep to themselves. Your turn now. What's the surprise you mentioned? My parents were saying that someone has donated a huge amount of money to the school. So maybe we can expect some...oh!'

Laila abandoned her sentence and started running. Over the lawn and cutting through the playing fields. She made for the back wall where there was a tall, rectangular netting cage. There was no grass inside it, but something that looked like a rough giant carpet was rolled up at one end. She went closer and nudged a pile of iron nails, each bigger than her hand.

She grinned as Shalini arrived, panting. 'I don't believe it!'

Shalini grinned back. 'Surprise!'

'Yes!' Laila cried. She caught Shalini's shoulders and twirled her around. 'Yes! Yes! We're having cricket at Rosebud. It's the best surprise! Ever!'

'I thought you'd like it. But what's the carpet thing?'

'It's the matting—for the wicket.'

Laila was silent for a few seconds. Cricket would never be the same for her after the...scandal. But she was surprised at how happy this had made her. Maybe they were two separate things.

Shalini was pulling her sleeve. 'What's the matter?'

'Nothing.' She shook herself. 'Come on, show me your room.'

Day scholars were not usually allowed in the hostel, but as term hadn't started yet, the rules were lax. They kept an eye peeled for teachers anyway, but the corridors were deserted.

Shalini's room was 213, on the second floor. They took the stairs two at a time and Shalini ushered her into a small but airy room at the end of the corridor. There were two lowish loft beds on two sides, each with storage space underneath. Each bed had a desk at right angles to it, along the wall. There was a large window above the desks, with a plain metal grill and a red-and-black checked curtain billowing in the breeze. Opposite the window, next to the door were a mirror and a set of shelves.

Shalini's side of the room was done up, with books on the desk, a mattress and sheets on the bed and a few odds and ends on the tackboard above the desk.

Laila looked around approvingly. 'I like this room. It's bigger than the one you had last year.'

'This is one of the new rooms. They've done up the whole school.'

'Lots of renovation going on in this town,' Laila observed, leaning out of the window. 'Nice view.'

Shalini grimaced. 'But I have a new roomie.'

'What? Why? No Prahati?'

She shook her head gloomily. 'They shuffle the boarders every year.'

'Who are you with?'

She shrugged. 'New girl. Forgot her name.'

Laila picked up a book lying face down on Shalini's bed. 'You're reading textbooks already?'

'I'm bored and the library is not open yet,' Shalini said, snatching her English reader from Laila and putting it under her pillow quickly. 'It's just stories. Come on, let's go to the kitchen and see if we can get a snack. They must be making a fancy lunch for the teachers' workshop.'

●

Laila's parents ran a laundry and dry-cleaning shop in the Central Market. Theirs was one of the oldest shops and the only dry-cleaners in town, so almost everyone got their carpets, blankets, coats and curtains cleaned there. Some days, on holidays and when she had time before school, Laila helped her father organize the day's pickups and deliveries. Her job was to check each list, ensure that the right things were going to the right places.

She also helped him separate the orders that were to be delivered from those that were to be collected.

That morning, Laila picked up a list and noticed the address—SJ House. Her curiosity was piqued. She'd already picked up some gossip—helping out in the shop as she did some evenings, she'd heard people talking about the town's latest residents. Or rather, *trying* to talk about them, because nobody seemed to know who they were. Nobody had seen them, nobody even knew their names.

'Do you think it's someone famous?' Laila had asked her mother one evening, when a particularly nosy neighbour had tried to ply them with questions.

'Why would someone famous want to come and live here?' her mother had asked back.

'I don't know—maybe to stay away from the media or something. Unless...'

'Unless what?'

Laila, who had seen a rather violent but exciting action movie on TV the previous night after her parents had gone to bed, said, 'Like the mafia or something.'

'Don't be silly.'

She checked their list with extra interest. There were lots of curtains—hardly surprising seeing how many windows the house had—a few heavy quilts, the kind that you only used during the winter, and a couple of silk saris. It wasn't particularly different from their other customers. So ordinary, it was almost boring.

'Abba, these new people at Old Mr Marshall's house, have you seen them?'

'No, why?'

'Just. I wonder if Sanjay Bhaiya has seen them.' Sanjay Bhaiya was their delivery van driver.

'Doubt it. Their caretaker drops and picks up their stuff. Why do you ask?'

'No reason. It's just peculiar that no one knows them, no one's seen them.'

'That's their business if they want to stay private. I hope you're not paying attention to the useless gossip.'

'No, Abba, of course not,' said Laila, as she knew she was supposed to.

●

Laila glanced at the noticeboard to see where her new classroom was before jogging up the stairs. Everything smelt fresh and clean. The class eight classroom was the first one to the right just off the landing. It was a big, wide room, looking out on to the playing fields (but not the cricket net, sadly). On one wall were rows of cubbyholes. The desks were arranged in a semicircle. There was a reading corner towards the back of the room, with a sparsely filled bookshelf—it would fill up soon with contributions from the girls.

'Hiii!' someone called out. It was Sophie, with her friend Rukmini.

'Hi,' Laila said. A couple of other girls came in and everyone exchanged excited notes about everything that was new and argued about which seats to take. One of the things Laila liked about Rosebud was that they were allowed to choose their own seats and even sit together with friends if they wanted.

'Four new girls,' Rukmini said, pointing to the class noticeboard. 'Look.'

Laila went to study the chart with her. She ran her eyes down the list and frowned. 'We're having *boys* now?'

'What, where?' Rukmini asked.

Laila pointed to one of the photographs, but by then she'd already read the name: Jasmine Barua. 'Oh.'

There was a flurry behind them—footsteps, voices, chairs being dragged. The rest of the boarders were streaming in. Laila locked eyes with a stranger—a tall girl with very short hair. But there was no mistaking Jasmine Barua. And from her glare, Laila was willing to put money on the fact that she'd heard her too. Drat.

Chapter 3

'Good morning and welcome back to a brand new school year!' Shirin Maneckshaw, principal of Rosebud Academy, detached the mic from its stand and took a little walk up and down the stage.

Aunty, as the students called her—it had started off as a nickname, but now everyone called her that openly—was in her fifties, with jet black hair done up in a plait as thick as Laila's arm that swung well past her waist, and she cut a rather larger-than-life figure on the whole. Rumour had it that in her younger days Aunty had once been a professional singer—she had a few Bollywood films under her belt—but had given it up for her first love, teaching. Indeed, she had a fascinating voice, clear and sweet and yet could, without warning, boom out, making you jump. But underneath her large and loud presence, she was quite a softy. Except when she lost her temper. Nobody wanted to be on her wrong side then.

'I'm sure all of you young ladies have had lovely summer holidays and are raring to jump straight into a very special year, with lots of new things to experience.'

Laila rolled her eyes at Shalini. Aunty always gave the same back-to-school speech every August at the start of the new school year, all about new beginnings—weren't all beginnings new?—and new challenges, and something that sounded like 'carpetiyum'.

'As most of you will have noticed,' she went on, sweeping her free arm in a wide arc, 'there have been many changes around here. The boarding house has been fully renovated and, of course, we have a brand new auditorium. And last but not least, Rosebud Academy will also be home to our town's first cricket coaching centre for girls.'

That generated a lot more excitement.

'We are honoured and privileged to have with us Ms S.M. Swapna, former Indian cricketer, as our coach.'

Laila drew her breath in sharply.

'Huh?' said Shalini.

'That's...she was the coach of the World Cup team! The women's team that was runner-up. And she's played for India.'

'Whoa, really?'

'Shh, let me listen!'

But Aunty had moved on to the twenty-six new students, fifteen in the fresh class six batch that had moved up from Rosebud Junior School on the other side of town, and eleven others, and how they must be made to feel welcome. There were some new teachers too whose names Laila didn't catch. But she noted that their Hindi teacher Madhuri Miss had become surprisingly skinny, Vinod Sir had a new haircut and Gayathri Miss looked more disgruntled than ever.

'I'm sure all of you are pumped up and can't wait to get the ball rolling on this wonderful new session,' boomed Aunty, 'but we must take a moment to thank our very generous benefactor, who wishes to remain anonymous. Suffice it to say that they are *very* keen to see us making best use of these wonderful opportunities that have been made available. And I'm sure that we will all rise to the occasion.'

With a needless scraping of chairs, everyone stood for the school song.

●

One of the new teachers, Shabnam Sodawalla, was their class teacher. She would also be teaching them English.

She looked barely older than Laila's sister, who was a college student, and kept adjusting her dupatta nervously as she introduced herself and asked the girls to tell her their names. Laila had a sense from the way Shilpa and Shilpi were giggling and nudging each other that they were going to give her a hard time. The two of them were known pranksters and while most of the other teachers had their antennas out for them, the new ones were always fair game.

But she did have exciting news.

'All of you will get a chance to be middle school prefects,' she announced. 'Two at a time, for one month.'

Shilpi raised her hand, eyes gleaming. 'Miss, can we give punishments?'

'Um…you will lead by example,' said Shabnam Miss. She rustled the pages of the attendance book. 'Shilpi Mathur, is that your…?'

'My what, Miss?' Shilpi was the picture of innocence.

Somebody giggled.

Shabnam Miss didn't reply. Instead, she placed a sheaf of class timetables on Shilpi's desk. 'Pass them out, please.' To the class, she said: 'As you know, every girl has to choose one sport and one hobby class. You can all decide and let me know in…soon.'

Then she turned, picked up the chalk and started to

write on the blackboard. The class groaned in protest.

'Miss, it's the first day!'

'Please, Miss, let's chat!'

Shabnam Miss turned around. 'What if we do some puzzles?'

'Yes, puzzles!'

So Shabnam Miss produced a stack of crossword puzzles and they spent the rest of the period solving them. It was only later that it struck Laila that they might have been tricked into doing vocabulary practice.

'Oh...my god...hurts!' gasped Sophie, clutching her side.

Second period was games with the new cricket coach, Swapna Miss. 'Come on, come on, keep running.' She clapped her hands. 'No stopping.'

'What's the point...of tiring us out...by making us run...round and round...the field?' panted Prahati. 'We'll be too pooped...to do anything...after that.'

Laila agreed, but there was no point wasting her breath in a reply.

Swapna Miss finally blew her whistle and they gathered, clutching various body parts, in the middle of the field. She took them through an elaborate set of stretches and loosening-up exercises. This was followed by a catching game—'Caterpillar Catch,' Swapna Miss called it—where they formed two lines facing each other, and threw a cricket ball from one side to the other in a zigzag form. She had a disconcerting habit of using articles in the wrong place: 'We make the friendship with ball.'

'I want to do batting and bowling,' muttered Laila grumpily as the hard leather-covered ball thudded into her hands and she bit her lip to stop herself from grimacing. 'Not make friendship with a stupid ball.' The damn thing *hurt*!

'Use the soft hands!' called Swapna Miss. 'Like I showed you. And remember, follow through.' She beckoned for Laila to throw the ball to her, and cupped her hands to receive it, almost gently, swinging her hands back. 'See? Welcome it into hands like this. Or else you will bruised very fast.'

All this was easier said than done. Laila, who had played a decent bit of roadside cricket herself had never in fact played with a real cricket ball. It was quite a shock for her to see how hard and heavy it really was.

After that they did some ground fielding—running after the ball or running forward and picking it up, and throwing it back at the stumps. Everybody got a chance to wear a pair of wicketkeeping gloves and stand behind the single stump to receive the throws. And there was more running and jumping and stretching.

'You said cricket was going to be fun,' Prahati complained as they trudged back, sweaty and aching.

'How is it my fault?' grumbled Laila. But Prahati was right. They hadn't even gone near the shiny new net yet.

●

'Exchange?' Nilofer pushed her tiffin box towards Shalini. They exchanged their snacks without a word. Laila exchanged hers with Prahati.

'Are we allowed to do that?' asked Davinder shyly. She and her twin Harminder were arguably the most exciting new girls in class, mainly because they looked absolutely, completely identical. Right from their skinny frames and long, neat plaits. They were boarders and had already earned the nicknames—Photo and Copy. Not that anybody could tell one from the other.

'Sure.' Prahati examined the insides of Laila's sandwiches. 'The day scholars always have more exciting tiffin.'

'I have fruit salad,' called Kanupriya from the twins' other side. 'Want to exchange?'

'No, thank you!' said Harminder hurriedly, though her sister looked mildly interested.

'So, Jas, where are you from?' Laila asked Jasmine,

still trying to assuage her guilt about the new girl.

'My name is Jasmine,' she replied in a flat voice.

'Oh, okay.' Under her breath to Prahati, she added, 'Geez.'

In a couple of days, they were already beginning to get a sense of the new students. Jasmine, for instance, was quiet to the point of being surly. She had a strange accent—when she did deign to speak—and didn't seem to care if anyone liked her. She kept to herself and rarely smiled. The only time she seemed to really enjoy herself was during games. She was a natural at sport, and Laila both admired and envied that. She was also Shalini's new roommate, who reported that Jasmine had barely spoken two sentences to her this past week.

The twins kept to themselves as well, but they were otherwise friendly. They were also terrified of the cricket ball, and Shalini said—out of their earshot, of course—that it made her nervous seeing them tottering uncertainly about during games period.

The fourth new girl, Sanya, was a day scholar. Though Laila had initially put her down as a giggly airhead, Rukmini informed them at the end of the first week that she was some sort of musical genius. Rukmini's mother taught music at Rosebud, which was where she got her information from.

Chapter 4

On Sunday afternoon, Laila was minding the shop and reading an old issue of *India Today* that she'd been avoiding for a while. It had an in-depth coverage of the match-fixing scandal that had stirred up Indian cricket a couple of months ago—a scandal that had at its centre star opening batsman Sunil Saifi, once the Indian team's captain and Laila's hero since the age of seven. In fact, he was the very reason she had even got interested in cricket. Saifi, along with three of his teammates, had been given a life ban from cricket and was now persona non-grata with the cricketing world at large, including the cricket-loving public, of course. There was even some court case pending against them.

Laila had long been in denial about her favourite

cricketer's new-found status as a cheat. 'How is it possible? Look at his record over the past two years—he's in great form and look at the team results!' she had complained to her father.

'I always thought he looked a bit shifty,' was all her father had to say.

The reporter who had done the *India Today* story, a well-known sports writer called G. Sharda, had a detailed explanation of how spot-fixing—the fixing of small events and not the result of a match—worked. Which meant that Saifi and his other guilty teammates were able to fix away to their heart's content without anybody getting suspicious until a bookie spilt the beans.

The fact that Sunil Saifi had admitted to everything meant that Laila had had to face the truth. Time was when she'd scoured the Internet for every bit of information she could get about him—including photos from his childhood in Australia. But now she avoided looking at the news for fear of finding out new horrible things about him. Lately she had even deactivated her Facebook account because she couldn't stand reading about Sunil Saifi in her timeline.

Suffice it to say, she was in a rather bad mood when she got to the bottom of G. Sharda's investigative story into 'Cricketgate'. 'What a stupid name. What does it even mean?' Laila said aloud as she smacked the magazine down on the pile of old newspapers for recycling. She considered reorganizing the old bill books drawer when a shadow fell across the counter.

Laila looked up in surprise. Sunday afternoons were always very slow. She didn't understand why her parents didn't just close the shop for a couple of hours. After all, who would have a dry-cleaning emergency at that time? But it was only Kartik Bawa—a local reporter who was always on the lookout for his next scoop to help him break into the national media. He usually wrote for the weekly *Chandnisarai Gazette*, making racy news items out of events like flower shows and school sports days.

Kartik lived in the next lane and regularly brought his sheets and blankets around for cleaning. Today he sauntered in holding a quilted jacket on a hanger. 'Your parents not around?' he asked, draping it on the counter.

'They're inside,' Laila responded. 'Do you want this dry-cleaned?' It looked perfectly clean to her, even pressed, but who was she to question a potential customer.

'Yes, please. How much will it be?'

Laila looked up the price list, calculated the discount for regulars and told him. Then she made out a receipt for him.

Kartik leaned on the counter as she wrote. 'So, do

you often help out in the shop?'

'Sometimes.'

'Interesting job this. Must be meeting lots of people.'

'Sure,' agreed Laila.

'You must be knowing almost everyone in town, no?'

'Well, not really,' said Laila. 'But yeah, most people get their stuff cleaned here, so...'

'Bet you know the names of the people who've just moved into Old Mr Marshall's place.'

She stared at Kartik. 'What?'

'Come on. Do you or do you not?' He winked conspiratorially. 'I have a bet with my colleague. I said, I'm hundred per cent sure Naushad-ji and family know everything that happens in town. And my friend didn't agree. So I bet him five hundred bucks that you lot know the name of the people. Come on, you do, right? Help me win!'

Some part of her was flattered that he thought she'd know. The rest of her was aware that she would probably be grounded for life if her parents found out that she was gossiping about customers—it wouldn't matter that she had no information about them whatsoever.

'I can't tell you.' Laila crossed her arms. 'Er... confidentiality purposes and all that, you know.'

'Ah, you're a tough nut to crack.' Kartik pursed his lips.

It looked completely theatrical. 'How about this. I'll tell you my theory—if it's true, you don't do anything. If it's false, you can laugh at me. Okay?' And without waiting for her to reply, he ploughed on. 'It's Pia Ghosh, right? With her new secret hubby in tow, Adil Khan?'

This time Laila's mouth fell open. Kartik had just named Bollywood's two hottest stars. There was a rumour that they'd got married in secret in Dubai or someplace. The only reason she knew this was because her sister Zainab had come home for the weekend and her slippers had been wrapped in a sheet of *HT City*, where the supposed wedding was a top story.

A couple of seconds later, Kartik jumped up and pumped a fist in the air. 'I knew it! I *knew* they were hiding out here!'

'Kartik Uncle...' Laila called after him, but he was already puttering away on his moped.

●

A couple of days later, when Laila reached her classroom, she found Sanya and two class nine girls bent over a newspaper, an air of excitement emanating from them.

'What's up?' she asked Shalini and Rukmini, who were looking on.

'PG and Adil Khan are hiding out in our town!'

Rukmini said. 'Did you know?'

'Did I know *what*?'

'The actress Pia,' explained Shalini with a grin. 'The *Gazette* says that's who's at Old Mr Marshall's place and that she's got married to...'

Laila groaned. 'Oh no. That's my fault.'

'What do you mean 'your' fault?'

'That idiot!' Laila went over and snatched the paper from Sanya. Sure enough, there was the byline, 'Special Correspondent Kartik Bawa', and he claimed to be quoting 'anonymous local sources'.

'Damn it!' Laila sat down at her desk, head in her hands.

'What do you have to do with PG's secret wedding?' Shalini demanded.

'You *know* PG and Adil Khan?' Sanya's eyes were round with new respect.

'No, no, I don't have anything to do with any Bollywood wedding!' cried Laila.

'Bollywood wedding?' Prahati asked with a laugh. The other boarders had started trickling in. 'Laila, what *have* you been up to?'

And so Laila told them about the little misunderstanding with Kartik Bawa. 'If my parents find out I was the 'anonymous source', they are going to kill me!'

'They think a Bollywood couple is secretly hiding in that house?' asked Jasmine.

That was the longest sentence Laila had hear her speak.

'Well, to be honest, we don't know that they aren't,' Kanupriya pointed out.

'Our mother's a journalist,' said Harminder. 'And she says that you always check and double-check facts. So this Kartik wasn't being a very good journalist if he only went by your word, Laila.'

'But I *didn't* give my word,' Laila insisted.

'Or maybe he checked and double-checked and PG and Adil are really staying there,' said Sanya.

Jasmine laughed. 'Seriously? You *think*?'

'You know better? You're not even from around here.'

Jasmine shook her head at Sanya and walked to her seat.

Shalini slipped into her seat. 'That Kartik Bawa is a complete cartoon.'

Laila couldn't agree more.

To their everlasting shock, class eight had discovered that Aunty was going to be teaching them social studies. What was even more shocking was that she turned out to be a rather interesting teacher.

They were studying the colonial period, the beginning of British rule, and she told them the story of how their town of Chandnisarai was born. In the mid-nineteenth century, it had only been a sleepy little village, until a major road was built and a caravanserai was set up here for travellers to break their journeys and rest overnight. A market came up soon after. This was followed by some major excitement here during the Rebellion of 1857, when most of the caravanserai was destroyed, but the area soon developed into a thriving market town.

'The reason I told you this story,' said Aunty, 'is so you know your town's history. So this semester, I want you all to do a project connected with the British period in Chandnisarai. It can be about an event or a location, or it can even be an object. Be creative, use your imaginations. The format is up to you. It can be a report, a presentation, a film—anything.

'You will work in groups of at least three. Take your time, do your *research*. You will all get a chance to present your ideas in class.'

●

'This school is obsessed with projects,' grumbled Prahati as they stretched out under their favourite tree after lunch.

'Mm,' said Laila, leaning back against the trunk, feeling deliciously lazy and also slightly regretting that second helping of rajma-rice. 'What shall we do ours on?'

'The Town Hall?' Shalini suggested half-heartedly.

'Too obvious,' Laila said.

'Wait a minute,' Prahati poked Laila, 'how old is your shop? Or else...oh, I know, how about the Parsi Colony? It's got some really old houses...and people.'

Laila shook her head. 'I already heard someone talking about it. The shop's not that old either. We should do something no one else will think of.'

'Should we get some more people in our group?' said Prahati.

'We could ask Photo-Copy. They seem the brainy types.'

Prahati nudged Shalini with the toe of her shoes. 'Earth to prefect!'

Shalini, who was taking her new status as prefect quite seriously, jumped. 'What?' She was kneeling on the grass, looking at something with great concentration.

'Shh, prefect on duty!' said Laila, and rolled away laughing as Shalini gave her a push. 'What *are* you staring at?'

'Just...noooo, don't look!'

Of course, that meant both Laila and Prahati turned

around. There were girls milling around everywhere in the grey and red uniform of Rosebud Academy. Most of them were walking or stretched on the grass, enjoying the last ten minutes or so of the lunch break. The younger ones were running around, screeching and laughing and playing.

'Are you watching Romi and gang?' asked Prahati.

Shalini turned to her. 'So you've heard too?'

'What are you talking about?' Laila interjected.

'You know Romi?'

'Yeah, the big bully from class nine, who pinches you if you pass too close to her. I pinched her back once last year and ran. What about her?'

'Well, I have a feeling she and her gang are troubling the new class six girls, but I haven't actually seen anything.'

'What happened to Aunty's strict anti-bullying policy in the hostel?' Laila asked.

'The kiddies are too scared to report them.'

Chapter 5

Bat and ball connected with a satisfying crack. Laila held her position at the end of her follow through and watched the ball streaking straight down the wicket, past the hapless bowler, who stuck out a foot—albeit a fraction too late—to stop it.

There was a cry of admonition from Swapna Miss. 'How many times I tell you girls NOT to do that!' She shook her head. 'All the bad habits from TV!' she muttered. 'Five rounds! New rule—stop ball with foot means five rounds.'

The bowler, Tara, who was one class below Laila, went off for her five rounds glumly. Laila went back to her stance as Shilpi tore in to deliver the next ball, her ponytail flying. Shilpi had discovered a love and a talent for pace bowling. The ball hurtled towards Laila's feet, and having learnt how much the damn thing hurt even through the pads and thigh pad, she feared for her toes. She tried to stick her back out, but the next thing she knew, the stumps were scattered.

The ball hit the net and rolled back towards her, and she threw it back to Shilpi. 'Who do you think you are, Dale Steyn?'

'We'll see,' Shilpi replied ominously.

When Laila took her stance again, Swapna Miss, who was 'umpiring'—also known as pointing out mistakes—called out, 'Left arm around.'

To Laila's surprise, there was Jasmine, swinging her arms around in a very professional, cricketer-y manner and tossing the ball from hand to hand. She took a short, four- or five-step run-up and bowled. The ball looped up and Laila, who had sensibly decided beforehand to defend, only realized much after the ball had passed her that it was a perfect good-length ball. It pitched and she brought bat and pad carefully forward to meet it, elbow up. But the moment the ball hit the ground, it veered away from her, missing the edge of her bat by a whisker and going harmlessly into the net behind.

'Shit!' said Laila before she could stop herself. What just happened? Had it *turned*?

Swapna Miss clicked her tongue. 'Not concentrating today? Last two balls.'

Later, when she had got out of her batting gear and was doing fielding drills with Rukmini (who, under pressure to participate in more extracurricular activities, had volunteered to join the cricket club and be a wicketkeeper because 'you basically have to stand behind the stumps all day'), Jasmine was batting in the nets. Laila stopped to watch her.

She batted left-handed and—well, there was no other way to say it—her timing and strokes were quite amazing. She had a far greater range of strokes than Swapna Miss, who set great stock by 'technique', had allowed the others to play so far. Laila almost held her breath as Jasmine executed a back-foot drive. Then she took a few steps forward and swatted an invisible pebble off the matting in a very proper batsman-like fashion. Laila made a mental note to try that sometime.

'Hello, the batters have run twenty by now!' Rukmini called out and Laila threw the ball back.

The Rosebud Cricket Club had been a hit in Chandnisarai. So much so, that there were two practice sessions—one early morning for girls from the town and one after school for Rosebud students. If all went well, Swapna Miss had promised there would be a match between the school and locals.

Laila, of course, had joined up and so had Prahati. Shalini had refused point-blank and was currently dithering between Computer Club and Art Club. But there were others from their class—Jasmine, for one, Shilpi and Nilofer, who were sporty types anyway, and, to everyone's surprise, the indolent Rukmini.

On their way back inside to change, Laila tried to talk to Jasmine again, 'Have you played for a team or something?'

Jasmine looked at her for a full five seconds before saying, 'Yes.'

That was all.

●

'Thanks to you, I'm a laughing stock in the journalistic community!' growled Kartik Bawa.

'It's not my fault! You ran off before I could say anything!' Laila looked around nervously for her father. He'd stepped into the storeroom while she lowered the shutters.

'We had a deal.'

'We had no deal. You lied to me to try and get information! That was sneaky.'

'I might lose my job. My editor is very upset!'

'It's not my fault you didn't check your facts,' said Laila. 'I'm shutting the shop. You have to go.'

Kartik pursed his lips. 'Laugh all you want, but I smell a story.'

'I'm not laughing.' Laila was very serious.

Kartik tapped the side of his nose. 'This is well-trained. It can sniff out things. That's an old house with a lot of history—it's where people go when they want to hide. You mark my words.'

Even though she didn't really want to talk to him, there was one thing Laila was curious about. 'What made you think it was Pia Ghosh hiding there?'

'Because she grew up in these parts. She has a family home in the city. And who else would come and sequester themselves here?'

'Oh, okay,' said Laila who had no idea what sequester meant. 'Good night, Kartik Uncle.'

The conversation with the bumbling reporter had planted the seed of an idea into Laila's head, but before she had a chance to talk to the others, Swapna Miss decided that they should have a practice match in a real cricket ground. That, of course, put all else out of her mind for a few days.

Since the school only had a training pitch, they

'borrowed' the Chandnisarai Sports Club's cricket ground for a few hours one afternoon. There were seventeen girls in the cricket club, but Laila roped Shalini in for the game so there was an even number.

It was to be a short ten-overs-a-side game. 'It's for you to get a feel of the match situation,' Swapna Miss said.

Jasmine and a class nine girl, Anju, were the two captains. Laila and Shalini were both in Jasmine's team, while Prahati ended up in Anju's.

Anju won the toss and decided to bat, but they only managed thirty-five runs in their ten overs. To Laila's surprise, Jasmine asked her to open the batting with Nilofer. She was pretty confident they'd get their thirty-six runs to win, but after Nilofer lobbed a catch back to the bowler and the number three, Tara, managed to get run out in the first three overs with just six on the board, her confidence plummeted into her shoes.

Jasmine came in at number four and things steadied for a bit. Two more overs went by and twelve runs were added—five of which came from a wide that went to the boundary. In the next over, Jasmine attempted a cut, but mistimed it. The ball went hard into the ground and bounced up into the air.

Laila heard a snigger from somewhere behind her. She turned around and saw a group of boys near the boundary.

Among them was her cousin, Murad, who went to the boys' school near Rosebud. She didn't know the others. One of them said something and the others laughed. She couldn't hear them, but it wasn't hard to guess why they were amused. She pointed a warning finger at Murad, but he just waved back, grinning cheekily.

Laila gritted her teeth, thinking of dire punishments for him, and turned back to the game. Jasmine was wearing a murderous frown. She made a signal to the umpire (Swapna Miss, of course) and gestured for Laila to meet her in the middle of the pitch.

'We are not going to let them think girls can't play cricket, are we?' Jasmine asked Laila.

'Not on your life!'

'Good. Just put bat to ball and try to keep it on the ground. Nothing fancy.'

Laila, fuelled with adrenaline, nodded, quite forgetting to be surprised that Jasmine was being normal.

But fancy it was! Jasmine came down the wicket to the next delivery and whacked the ball straight. It went up in the air—safely—and smacked into the white concrete wall of the clubhouse that served as a sightscreen.

Laila didn't hear a single snigger or giggle after that. When she got the strike and easily swept a short ball through midwicket, where the boys were all sitting on the ground, watching the game in silence. They even cheered when the ball crossed the boundary. In the end, Laila's team got their thirty-six runs with seven balls to spare.

'Nicely done,' Murad called when the match was over and they were packing up.

'I know,' shot back Laila, adding, 'Thanks to you,' under her breath. Jasmine heard her and snorted with laughter.

Laila looked at her, grinning. 'That was fun.'

'Yeah.' She took off her cap, shook it and put it back on again.

Laila frowned.

'What?'

'Nothing. You…just…sometimes you remind me of someone. I feel like I might have seen you somewhere.'

'In school every day?'

'No, I mean from before.'

Jasmine shrugged and didn't say another word on their way back to school.

●

'Let's do the project on Old Mr Marshall's house,' Laila said to the others the day after the match.

'That decrepit old house?' Prahati asked.

'I know, I know, but listen—it's what that Kartik Bawa said, that it's an old house with a lot of history. I asked my dad and he confirmed that the house was originally built in the nineteenth century, so we have the right period. There are so many stories about it, how it's cursed and about Mr Marshall himself. There's a statue of him on Mall Road, even. So it's clearly an important monument in Chandnisarai's history.'

'And,' put in Shalini with a grin, 'it might give the three of us a chance to actually solve the mystery of its current occupants.' The twins had been 'taken', so it was just the three of them on the project.

'Exactly!'

'You really hope to find Pia Ghosh and Adil Khan dancing around trees in there?'

'I still think the Parsi Colony idea is better,' Shalini said.

Laila shook her head. 'Another group is doing the Parsi Colony. Anyway, remember that roadside inn that Aunty was telling us about, the caravanserai?'

'What about it?' Shalini asked.

Laila, who was saving her trump card just in case, decided to play it. 'Well, it was located on the grounds of the house. Also, my grandmother says revolutionaries used to hide there before Independence.'

Chapter 6

'Laila, you have visitors,' her mother called.

Laila looked up in surprise—half terrified that it was Kartik Bawa again, about to get her into trouble. But it was only Murad, and he had brought another boy.

'This is my friend Samir.'

'Hi,' said Laila. 'Weren't you there during our practice match the other day?'

Samir said hi back and nodded in reply. He seemed a little shy.

'So all this cricket-shicket, huh?' said Murad. 'Awesome.'

Laila shrugged modestly. 'Nah. We've been playing for years. In Nani's yard, remember?'

'Yeah, but that was just messing about.'

She grinned. 'That's true. Remember how we used the big flowerpot as a wicket?'

'Those were fun days.'

Laila and Murad had been born a few months apart—their mothers were sisters—and for a long time they'd been playmates. They'd gone to the same school—Rosebud Junior School, which was coed—till they reached class six.

'Yeah, but then you disappeared,' said Laila.

'So did you.'

That was true too. Laila had made friends with Shalini and Prahati, and didn't really have time for Murad any more. She'd always told herself that he preferred to hang out with the boys from his school.

'Do you want Tang?' she asked to change the subject.

They did and they all trooped to the kitchen to get some.

'So, Samir wants to ask you something,' said Murad after they'd got their cold drinks.

Samir looked terrified. 'I thought you'd ask!' he told Murad.

'No way!'

'Please.'

'Forget it.'

'What?' asked Laila impatiently.

'Can I,' began Samir haltingly, 'do a...biographyofyou?'

'A what?'

'He means a biography,' explained Murad. 'It's for an English project. We have to write a biography of a real person.'

'Does your school get ideas from Aunty?' asked Laila.

'What?'

'Never mind. Sure, Samir. What do I have to do?'

Samir, who had gulped down his Tang in one go, and was now looking rather red, stared disbelievingly at Laila. 'Oh. Um, can I interview you?'

'Now?'

'No, no.'

'Okay.' To be honest, Laila felt rather flattered to be asked to be the subject of a biography. 'When?'

'I, um, will WhatsApp you?'

'I don't have a mobile phone.' She didn't add 'any more'. It had been taken away after she'd spent too much time talking with Shalini and run up a huge bill.

'You don't have a mobile phone?' echoed Murad incredulously.

'Why don't you email me?' Laila said, ignoring him.

Samir typed in her email ID on his mobile phone. 'Okay, thank you. I'll mail. Bye! ComeonMurad!'

And with that, he almost ran out of the room, dragging Murad with him.

Laila stared at the two of them in surprise. Were teenage boys generally mad or was it just this one?

Twenty minutes later, the landline rang. She answered and it was Murad.

'Thought I should explain,' he said. 'Samir likes you.'

'Ew!' cried Laila and banged down the phone.

'What happened?' her mother asked.

'Nothing!'

●

Laila sighed at the search results on the screen. 'That's not very helpful.'

'Why don't *you* try?' Shalini said, somewhat testily.

'Can I help you?' a grown-up voice asked behind them.

It was Gayathri Miss, their computer teacher, looking as grumpy as ever.

'Miss, it's possible to find anything on the Internet, isn't it?' asked Prahati.

'It could be, but it depends. What are you looking for?'

They told her about their history project. 'We want to find out about the history of Old Mr Marshall's place,' Laila explained. 'It was called Flycatcher Mansion before the current owners took it over.'

'But we haven't been able to find much,' Shalini added. 'There's nothing online. It was only in the news some eight, nine years back, when there was a robbery in the market and the police found the stolen goods there and the thieves' hideout.'

'My father says that after that incident, a caretaker was employed for a while,' Laila put in. 'But he isn't sure who actually owned the place. Or who's bought it right now.'

'Hmm.' Gayathri Miss's brow creased. 'So you don't buy the Pia Ghosh story?'

They stared at her in surprise.

'No miss!' said Laila, offended.

Gayathri Miss's mouth twitched in a smile. Had she made a joke? 'I think perhaps the Town Hall would be a better place to search than Google. Or the newspaper office. There was a time when the *Chandnisarai Gazette* was a serious newspaper, I'm told. They're bound to have records.'

'Could we ask Kartik Bawa?' wondered Laila.

'Yeah, right,' scoffed Shalini.

'No, silly, I meant, ask him if the paper has records.'

'Will you go and talk to him then?' Prahati asked.

'Ooh, that might be tricky,' said Laila. 'I bet he's still mad at me. Maybe one of you guys should get in touch. His email ID must be in the paper or on their website.'

'Or we can always land up at the *Gazette*'s office,' Prahati said

'If we're landing up, why not go straight to the house itself?' Shalini put in.

'Because Phoolchand is just going to intercept us again,' said Laila glumly.

'Who's Phoolchand?'

'The caretaker.'

'We're not trying to break in,' argued Shalini. 'We only need to look around the grounds.'

'And take some photos of the ruins.'

'There are ruins?'

'Yeah.'

'How do you know? You've been in there?' Prahati asked.

'Many times. We used to sneak in when we were kids, my cousin and I, pretending to be explorers. There was a different caretaker then and he didn't say anything. Later, I used to go by myself too.'

'Imagine,' said Shalini, staring dreamily into space, 'hundreds of years ago, all this must've been wilderness, even where we are standing, and weary travellers would probably see the lights of the inn from between the trees after a long day's journey. It'd be like finding an oasis in the desert...'

'Do you think they had electricity then?' Laila interrupted.

'What? Oho, you're spoiling the mood!'

●

'Wow, look at that!' cried Romi, pointing towards the sky.

Tanvi, the petrified class six girl, on whose shoulder Romi had planted her hand, looked up. Quick as a flash, one of Romi's two cronies bent down and yanked the youngster's track pants down to her knees. The trio hooted with laughter as the girl dropped the books she was carrying, struggling to pull up her tracks.

It had all happened so fast that Laila, who had been crossing the quadrangle between the hostel and the school building, found herself frozen in place.

By the time she roused herself, the seniors had already taken off, laughing like it was the funniest thing on earth.

Laila ran to Tanvi to help her pick up the books she had dropped. 'You okay?'

She nodded, but her lips were trembling.

'I saw everything,' said Laila angrily. 'I'm going to report them.'

'No, please!' Tanvi grasped Laila's sweater sleeve. 'Please don't. If you report them and they think it's me or one of my friends, it's going to get worse!'

'Listen, this is wrong. They are not allowed to bully you.'

'It's not a big deal. Please, don't tell anyone. Please, promise.'

Laila looked at the terrified little girl's face. 'Okay, fine.'

Tanvi scuttled away and Laila continued towards the school building, shaking her head. Was there a line between having some fun and bullying? she wondered. It hadn't looked like Tanvi had been having much fun.

The grounds and classrooms were deserted—there was another half an hour till assembly. Her footsteps echoed as she walked towards the staircase. Some cleaning staff apart, the building seemed to be deserted. She stood in the hall outside the principal's office, taking in the silence, almost spooky. There was a sudden burst of faint laughter from somewhere far away, probably the hostel. Then she heard voices, voices that were definitely coming from one of the rooms around her.

Curious to see who else might have come to school so early, she went to investigate. The door to the middle school staffroom was open. Shabnam Miss was seated at a table, with Aunty opposite her. They were talking earnestly, but in low voices so Laila couldn't make out the words clearly. She hadn't really meant to eavesdrop—and had *no* intention whatsoever of Aunty even suspecting that she might be trying to do so. She turned to go, when she heard Shabnam Miss say Shalini's name.

At that moment, Aunty noticed the movement out in the corridor and turned towards her, eyebrows quizzically.

'Er, good morning Miss,' mumbled Laila.

'Good morning,' Shabnam Miss responded. 'You're very early, aren't you?'

'I left my maths book... I have homework.'

'All right, carry on, then.'

Laila was keen to tell Shalini all about the incident with Romi and company, but Shalini didn't turn up in school that day.

'She's indisposed,' said Shabnam Miss when Laila asked. She wondered if that's why their class teacher had talking to Aunty about her.

'Is she going to be okay?' Laila asked, suddenly worried.

Shabnam Miss gave her a measured look. She opened her mouth as if to say something, but thought better of it. 'She's spending a couple of days with her parents. She'll be fine, nothing to worry.'

With no Shalini to co-opt, Laila told Prahati about what had happened, as they stood at the corner of the auditorium, watching Romi, Sheena and Deepa, sitting on the lawn, tiffin boxes open between them.

'So, is this a stakeout?' asked Prahati.

'I don't know,' said Laila irritably.

'You know, you can't keep following them around,' Prahati pointed out.

'I have to do *something*. I was such an idiot. I was right there, but I just froze.'

'Don't beat yourself up,' Prahati said. 'There were three of them. They're bigger than you.'

'If you know they're bullying the kids, why don't you do something?' Laila demanded. 'Report them?'

'Because,' said Prahati patiently, 'they're really good at what they do. They're clever and sneaky and mean. No one's ever caught them and they have the sixths terrified.'

'Isn't ragging illegal or something?' Laila asked. 'I read in the papers. Can't you tell Gayathri Miss? She's your warden, isn't she?'

'No, I can't. It'll be my word against theirs.'

Chapter 7

During cricket practice that afternoon, they did Caterpillar Catch with two balls, which was much trickier than it seemed, and Laila dropped so many catches that even Swapna Miss got sick of sending her for rounds and just ignored her.

Since Laila didn't bowl, after her stint in the nets, she joined the group that was doing ground fielding in the big field. Running after a ball that was racing to the boundary, she noticed one of the twins on the bench at the edge of the field.

'Hello,' she panted, picking up the ball and hurling it back to Rukmini who was standing behind a single stump that seemed a thousand kilometres away. 'Want to do some fielding?'

The girl—Laila couldn't tell which one of the twins it was—smiled. She was holding a book, but didn't seem to be reading.

Some time later, Swapna Miss sent the ball soaring into the air instead of along the ground. Shilpi, whose turn it was, ran to intercept it, but it was clear she would struggle to reach it. Meanwhile, it seemed to be coming straight down over Harminder/Davinder.

'Photo-Copy, look out!' someone yelled.

But Photo—or Copy—was already looking out. To Laila's surprise, instead of ducking, the girl jumped up and readied herself for a catch.

The ball smacked into her hands. Laila winced, knowing how much that must have hurt, and especially because she hadn't used 'the soft hands', one of Swapna Miss's favourite phrases.

'Well done!' Swapna Miss called, though she would have lambasted any of the others if they'd caught the ball that way.

Davinder—which Laila only found out later—grinned happily.

●

When Laila arrived in school the next day, she found Prahati waiting for her in a state of great excitement.

She held up a thin, dull-looking book. 'We were so caught up in doing things the high-tech way, we completely forgot about the school library.' The book was titled *Heritage Buildings of Chandnisarai*, written by a local historian called Professor Avinash K. Pradhan.

'And is Mr Marshall's house in it?' Laila asked.

'It is! Though there's not much.'

But it was a far sight more than what they knew so far. It all started with the roadside inn called Chandni Sarai. Like Aunty had said, it was a rest stop for travellers, with rooms to rest in, a place to rest their animals and eat. Unfortunately, the original caravanserai was all but destroyed during the 1857 Rebellion, when the British came after some fleeing soldiers they thought were hiding there. Later, a minor noble acquired the land and rebuilt the inn and also got a small palace built for himself, called Chandni Mahal. A market and a village grew around it, collectively known, again, as Chandnisarai. But they already knew most of this, as Aunty had told them.

For a long time, nothing exciting happened here. Then, in the early twentieth century, when the independence movement started hotting up, Chandni Mahal then was supposed to be a place where revolutionaries were provided shelter. It was said that those who came to hide here were never caught and never seen again.

'That sounds sort of spooky,' said Laila.

'It is rather,' said Prahati. 'Read on.'

Professor Pradhan went on to say that nobody ever knew whether these people managed to escape into the surrounding forests through the underground passages rumoured to run from beneath the house or whether they came to a more gruesome end.

In 1945, Chandni Mahal was 'acquired' by the Marshalls, and they stayed on in India even after Independence. Sir William Marshall was a keen ornithologist and named the place Flycatcher Mansion. However, it wasn't a very lucky place for him. There was a fire in the nursery in 1951, where his young children died. His wife never recovered and also died a few years later. That's what led the townspeople believe the house was cursed. After Old Mr Marshall—as he was called by then—died, his nephew moved in and ran Flycatcher Mansion as a hotel for a short time and then a retirement home, but nothing worked out, and the house eventually fell into disrepair.

'This book was written in 2003, so it's more than ten years out of date,' Prahati pointed out. 'But this Professor Pradhan lives here in town.'

'Cool. We could go visit him,' said Laila. 'By the way, where's Shalini? Have you seen her?'

Prahati nodded, then looked behind her like she was expecting Shalini to pop out. She lowered her voice. 'I don't know what's wrong with her. She isn't talking to me.'

●

Prahati had to go back to the hostel to get a book she had forgotten, so Laila went up to class alone. She kept a lookout for Shalini, but instead found Shabnam Miss waiting to announce that there was going to be an extended assembly for the middle school after the regular morning assembly. The girls trailed out after her. Not all of the boarders were in and Laila couldn't spot Shalini.

After the assembly, when the rest of the school had filed out, Aunty's assistant and Gayathri Miss set up a projector.

'What's going on?' Kanupriya whispered.

But nobody knew. And then—horrors! Aunty was holding up a sanitary pad.

'Oh my god, what is she doing?' murmured Prahati as a collective gasp went around the room.

Aunty gave it a wave. 'Is there *anyone* in this room who doesn't know what this is?' she asked.

Deathly silence followed. Laila wondered if, like her, all the others were trying to sink under their chairs. It was as if they were all trying not to breathe, so Aunty would think they weren't there and stop this excruciating exercise of embarrassing everyone to death.

'So, I'm assuming that's a no,' she went on. 'Which is a relief. It would be quite alarming if a school FULL OF ADOLESCENT GIRLS couldn't identify a sanitary pad!' She gave a small laugh, but nobody joined her. Shabnam Miss and two of the middle school class teachers, smiled. Even Gayathri Miss looked vaguely amused. Laila noted (thankfully!) that Vinod Sir was not there.

Despite the fact that there was a projector mounted on the ceiling that threw the words 'Health and Human Development' on a large screen behind Aunty, she launched into a peculiar speech about the flowering of buds and the turning of caterpillars into beautiful butterflies.

'What's happening?' Prahati hissed at Laila desperately.

'I don't know!' She threw a glance at Shalini, who was staring ahead impassively. She didn't look ill, but she did seem to be ignoring them.

'The human body is a miracle,' Aunty gushed, 'the way it changes and turns girls and boys into women and men is one of nature's enduring marvels. Can anybody tell me what this process is called?'

Apparently nobody could, but it didn't put Aunty off her stride. 'Puberty, of course! You have all heard about puberty, right?'

There were some half-hearted murmurs. The slide changed. It now said: 'Girls and Puberty: Everything You Need to Know about Body Changes and Other Stuff.'

'We have *Internet*—we know this stuff!' Laila whispered.

'Yeah, but I don't think Aunty knows that,' Prahati whispered back.

They listened to her go on about breasts and body hair and menstrual cycles in silence. After a while, a disembodied voice called out, 'Tell us about boys, Miss!' and everyone laughed.

Only Shalini didn't. Laila tried to catch her eye, but she continued to stare ahead, hardly seeming to pay attention.

●

Aunty was quite happy to give Shalini and Prahati a day pass from the hostel to meet Professor Pradhan. She only made them promise not to hound the old man in case he didn't want to speak to them.

'We can go Saturday morning, can't we?' asked Prahati.

Laila shook her head. 'Can't. I have to help in the shop. What about late afternoon, around four? Oh no, I have to meet Samir.'

'Who?' asked Prahati.

'Just this...a classmate of my cousin's.'

'A *boy*?'

'Yeah, it's not a crime, you know,' said Laila, trying to be offhand, but obviously failing, because they pounced on her. Even Shalini seemed interested.

'Where are you meeting him?'

'Ooh, is he your *boyfriend*?'

'Were you going to tell us?'

'Stop it!' said Laila, irritated. 'They have to do a biography of someone in town. So he asked my cousin if he could interview me. So I'm meeting him. So...that's it. Now stop being silly about it.'

'Interesting.' Shalini narrowed her eyes. 'So, basically, you have a date?'

'Argh! No! It's not like that. They were at our cricket match last week.'

'Aha, the one you were talking to!' cried Prahati. 'The dorky one?'

'No, that was my cousin. Now can we please talk about our project?'

'I think your date is much more interesting,' said Shalini with a grin. Laila reached across to slap her playfully, relieved that she seemed like her usual self. She hopped out of the way, laughing.

'Okay, get serious now,' Laila said. 'Since you already have a day pass, you could go and meet the professor by yourself. Do you know where he lives?'

Shalini and Prahati looked at each other. 'We thought you'd know.'

Laila groaned.

'I have an idea,' Prahati said. 'Let's go and see if we can find anything in the Town Hall on Saturday. We'll go see Professor Pradhan another day.'

Chapter 8

'I'm not very interesting, I don't know why you want do a biography of me,' said Laila.

'We are supposed to pick someone ordinary,' replied Samir. His eyes widened in shock immediately as he realized what he'd said. 'Sorry, I didn't mean that you were boring or anything!'

'It's fine.' But she was slightly stung anyway.

She had agreed to meet him in Chandnisarai's new coffee shop called Conversations. It was not a very apt name because the music was so loud, you could barely hear yourself think. Also, everything was very expensive. Laila had ordered the cheapest thing on the menu, which turned out to be black coffee and was revolting, even after emptying four sachets of sugar in it.

Samir stared down at his notebook, the tips of his sticky-out ears bright red. Laila wished she'd asked Murad to come. Finally, she said, 'I have to go somewhere after this, so...'

'Yeah, okay, sorry.' He uncapped his pen. 'When and where were you born?'

'January 2001 at Hill View Nursing Home.'

'Your family...?'

'Owns the laundry place. It was started by my father's uncle in...well, I don't know.'

'Brothers, sisters?'

'One sister. Nineteen. She's in college in Delhi.' Laila was starting to feel somewhat silly. Having to shout out her answers over the music wasn't helping. 'Listen, this is nuts. Can we go somewhere else? Maybe the park or back to my house.'

Samir looked rather relieved himself. 'Okay.'

They paid—Laila tried not to feel upset about how little change she got back—and went out into the dusk.

'Who's Murad doing his project on?' she asked.

'I don't know,' said Samir. They walked in silence and then he said. 'Look, no offence, but can you tell me something interesting about yourself?'

'I told you, I'm not very interesting.' They were passing the statue of Sir William Marshall on the other end of the

Mall Road. Laila pointed at it. 'We're tracing the history of his house for a school project.'

'Isn't that the house where Adil Khan is living?'

'You don't seriously believe that, do you?'

Samir looked a bit embarrassed. 'Not me, but some of the boys from my class hang around outside sometimes, hoping to catch sight of him. Or more likely they want to catch a glimpse of Pia Ghosh.'

'Murad and I used to sneak into the grounds to play when we were kids. They're huge. There are ruins there too. I wish we could explore inside, take a few photos and stuff, but that caretaker, Phoolchand, he's such a grouch that I'm afraid he'll say no just for the heck of it and won't even ask the owners for permission.'

'Yeah. He chased some boys from my class with a stick because they were taking photos.'

'Have your friends ever seen anyone there?'

Samir shook his head. 'There's a silver Honda City with tinted windows that comes and goes sometimes.' He seemed to know a great deal for someone who claimed not to have an interest.

'I know, I've seen it too,' said Laila. 'I was there when it first arrived with the house's new residents.'

'You saw them when they arrived?' asked Samir, eyes wide.

'Yep. I even went up to the house to try and see if I could say hello.'

'Cool! So you've seen them?'

Laila made a face. 'Well, yes and no. I saw one old woman, but there were two other people who got out of the car. They were on the other side, though, so I couldn't get a good look. I think at least one was a man—he was wearing a hat. The other person was shorter, probably a kid. I spoke to the driver, who called them "Bhaiya" and "Baby", but he was new, so he didn't know their names or anything.'

'Seems like you know a lot more than anyone else around here,' Samir said.

'I guess. But I can definitely tell you one thing—they were not Adil Khan and Pia Ghosh. I'm sure even the new driver would have recognized them.'

'Maybe not. Famous people look really different in real life, especially film stars because they wear so much make-up on screen.'

'Okay, but then who was the old woman and who was this Baby?'

Samir had to admit he didn't know. But he had an idea: 'Let's walk over and take a look?'

Solid wrought iron sliding gates towered over then. 'These are new,' observed Laila.

'And just in case they thought you were tall enough to climb over, they've put those spiky things on top too,' observed Samir.

'That's not all.' She pointed to a white spout-like thing mounted on a pole at one of the gateposts. 'I think that's a CCTV camera.'

There was a smaller, person-sized door in the gates. Laila gave it an experimental knock and Samir dragged her back.

'What are you *doing*! They can see you!'

'I was thinking, if Phoolchand opens the door, we can tell him that we're doing some school work and want to ask permission to explore the grounds.'

'If Phoolchand sees one more school kid, he's going to have a stroke. And anyway, I don't think that's how this works.' He pointed to a small console set into the gatepost, the same one that had the camera mounted, with a number pad and a metallic mesh-like rectangle above it.

'An intercom,' said Laila. 'I've seen these things in movies. They *really* don't want anyone to...'

There was a crackle of static from the speaker.

'Yes, who's there?' came an impatient voice.

The two of them turned around and fled.

They only stopped, out of breath, when they were safely far, far away.

'If you want to find out about the house, you should talk to Avinash Uncle,' said Samir, panting, hands on knees. 'He knows everything about the history of this town.'

Laila grabbed his arm. 'You mean Professor Avinash Pradhan? You *know* him?'

Samir nodded. 'He's my grandfather's childhood friend. Why?'

'Wow, this is a seriously small town!'

'Thanks to Laila's boyfriend, we have an appointment with Professor Pradhan next Saturday,' Shalini informed Prahati as they walked towards the hall for assembly on Monday morning.

'He's not my boyfriend!' said Laila with gritted teeth. 'Samir's grandfather and Professor Pradhan were school friends, so he got his granddad to call up and ask if he'd meet us.'

'And he said yes?'

'Yes. We also went up to the house to see if we could spot anything.'

'Oho, having adventures with your new boy...' Prahati started, but stopped when she saw Laila's murderous expression. 'And?'

Laila told them about the new gates and the intercom. 'They seem totally paranoid. Did you find any information at the Town Hall?'

'It was Saturday, so it was shut,' said Prahati. 'But...' She made a flourishing gesture towards Shalini, who continued.

'So, we decided to try our luck at the *Chandnisarai Gazette*.'

'We met the editor, who was very helpful. She even put us in touch with Kartik Bawa,' Prahati said.

'What did he say?' asked Laila.

'He said that about ten years back, the house was sold by the Marshall family to a trust called the Taleem Foundation. They wanted to open a school there, but they never got around to it. Something about not getting permission. He said, as far as he knows, the house still belongs to them.'

'He also said that loads of celebrities—film stars, cricketers, etcetera—have donated money to the Taleem Foundation,' Shalini added. 'Including Pia Ghosh, who gave a bundle last year and has also been doing promotional work for them. That was another reason he thought she could be here since, apparently, she's dropped off the radar after her wedding.'

'Yep, and we also saw the microfilm records of the *Gazette*,' Prahati put in. 'But the paper was shut down for about three, four years in the middle and after that it became a weekly, so there wasn't much. We didn't find any mention of the house.'

Chapter 9

During the history period, Aunty decided that each group should tell the rest of the class the topics they'd chosen and why. Rukmini, Nilofer, Kanupriya and Sophie went first. They had, in fact, picked the Parsi Colony, which wasn't surprising because Nilofer lived there. The twins, Jasmine and Sanya were doing theirs on the Mall Road. The remaining four had decided on the Glen Hotel, the oldest hotel in the town, mostly because Vidya's father was the manager there.

Laila, Prahati and Shalini were the last to present. There were some grins and sniggers when they revealed their subject.

'You just want to find out if film stars are staying there!' Shilpi cried out.

'No!' shot back Laila, stung by the implication. 'We have no interest in who is in the house. We just want its history.'

'Ha, just an excuse.'

'Your subject is rubbish!' Prahati shot back.

'Girls!' Aunty cut in. 'Simmer down. You've all picked wonderful ideas. In fact, having listened to all of you, I think we should have an exhibition for Parents' Day so they can learn a bit more about this town that you live in. I'm pleased with all your hard work so far. But now it's time to think about how you're going to do your research and how you're going to present your reports.'

'Give us some ideas, Miss,' Sanya said.

'No. I want you all to brainstorm and come up with your own formats. After the midterm break I want to hear your ideas.'

'You guys go on, I'll catch up.' Laila dabbed at the pool of water on her desk with the edge of her shirt. She'd knocked the flower vase over from the window next to her, but thankfully, it hadn't got on any of her books. She found an old tissue in her bag, which she spread on her desk.

'Why did you pick that house?'

Laila, who had been sure she was the only one in the classroom, looked up, startled.

It was Jasmine, her face black as thunder, eyes blazing.

'What?' said Laila.

'There are dozens of buildings in this town,' she growled. 'Why did you pick *that* house?'

Laila stared, speechless.

'Pick another house,' went on Jasmine, putting her hands on her hips belligerently.

Laila, who wasn't usually easily riled, found herself bristling. 'Mind your own business.'

But Jasmine only looked angrier. 'No, *you* mind your own business!'

'Eh? That doesn't even make sense. What's your problem?'

'My problem is that you think it's okay to snoop and pry.'

'Are you mad?' said Laila. 'Nobody's snooping and prying. Now are you going to get out of my way or are you going to continue standing there like a goonda?'

'Not till you pick another topic!'

'*You* pick another topic!'

'Girls? Is everything all right?' Shabnam Miss was standing at the door, looking at them questioningly.

Jasmine turned around and walked out of the room

without a word. Laila stared after her with her mouth open.

●

At first, Prahati didn't believe her. 'You're joking!'

'You can go ask her yourself,' said Laila. 'And while you're at it, you could perhaps also ask her why she's so upset about it.'

'She *threatened* you?' Shalini asked, equally doubtfully. 'I mean, sure, she's rather moody, but she's sort of okay otherwise.'

'Fine, I'm making it up!' Laila snatched up her tiffin box and got up.

'No, no, don't go!' cried Prahati. She caught Laila's arm and pulled her back down. 'It's not that we don't believe you. It's just so…weird. I mean, she threatened you about a class project?'

'She didn't exactly threaten me,' said Laila. 'Just accused me of snooping and that I should—we should—pick another house or else.'

'Or else what?' laughed Prahati. 'Chop us into tiny pieces and mail us to our parents?'

The others stared at her.

'But why?' asked Shalini. 'Why is *she* so interested in what we do our project on?'

'She's insane?' Laila offered. 'You'd better keep a knife under your pillow, Shalini.'

'Maybe she knows something,' said Shalini, 'about the house and doesn't want us to find out.'

'Yeah, right,' scoffed Laila. 'You read too many books.'

'And you were just telling me to keep a knife under my pillow?'

'Hush, you two, let me think,' said Prahati, waving her hand at them. 'We already know that whoever's living there is quite secretive. And Jasmine doesn't want us to snoop. Now, there are two possibilities. She's either doing it out of the goodness of her little heart...'

'Or, she knows who those people are and doesn't want anyone to find out,' finished Laila. 'Right?'

'It makes sense, but also it doesn't,' argued Shalini. 'How would she know? She's not even from around here... oh!' She gripped Laila's arm.

'Ow! What?'

'But she does know! I'm sure she knows!'

'How are you sure?'

'Remember the time when Kartik Bawa's article appeared in the *Gazette*? She was really amused. Like she *knew* it wasn't them.'

'So how *does* she know?' Laila asked.

Nobody had an answer to that.

Professor Pradhan lived in a rather fancy apartment complex at the edge of town. His flat, however, was dingy, stuffy and smelt of old people.

'It's Iodex,' Prahati whispered to Laila when she pointed that out.

The professor himself was a withered old man who looked like he might be swept away by the breeze from the fan. There were books everywhere in his living room, including on the floor. The woman who let them in, probably his daughter, didn't look terribly thrilled to see them, but she did clear newspapers from the sofa and brought in another chair so they could all sit. Later, she also got them Rooh Afza milkshakes with straws in them.

Professor Pradhan was an extremely garrulous old man. He launched off on how hard he had worked to keep the history of the town alive. 'I've crawled on my hands and knees,' he said at the end of his opening monologue, thumping his cane on the floor. 'I've climbed roofs and walls. I have gone all the way to Delhi to trace owners. And what do I have to show for it? Nothing. *Nothing*! This town is ungrateful. Ungrateful, I say!'

He stopped, out of breath. Prahati's straw made a slurping sound.

'So, er, we're doing...tracing the history of the old Flycatcher Mansion,' said Laila, realizing she'd better state their objective before he started off again.

'Yes, yes, you must tell everyone!' Professor Pradhan sounded excited. 'Tell everyone about that house. Great old house. From the time this place was a forest.'

'Please tell us about it, sir,' said Shalini meekly.

He was only too glad to oblige. For the next half an hour he held forth, but he really didn't have much more to add to what they already knew. Of course, he had details, like the name of the prince who rebuilt the house after 1857, names of the revolutionaries who were known to have hidden there and when. They dutifully noted all this down, but it was beginning to sound deathly dull to Laila. She stifled a yawn.

'Sir, what about the secret passages?' Shalini asked. 'Weren't there three of them?'

The professor nodded. 'You're quite right. Three of them, but only two of them were ever found. One from the house into the forest and one from the grounds of the house into the mountains. There was supposed to be another one from the court to the cellars of Chandni Mahal. Some prisoners were said to have gone missing from the holding cells in the court just before their cases came up before the magistrate. Nobody ever found out how they escaped. There were no signs of a breakout and no secret passage was found either.'

The girls looked at each other with shining eyes. 'Is it the same District Magistrate's Office on Mall Road?' Laila asked.

'Oh no. That building was torn down long ago. It's exact location was actually closer to the Town Hall. If you must know, I think this is just a story, that there never was any secret passage. It is more likely the guards in the court house were bribed.'

'Do the secret passages still exist?' asked Laila.

'Well, I suppose technically they probably do, but they were sealed off when the Marshalls bought the place.'

After leaving Professor Pradhan's house, they walked to Laila's place to brainstorm about how they would present it. They sat on Laila's bed and made points.

'I think our topic is pretty solid,' said Shalini. 'The house ties in very nicely to the history of Chandnisarai.'

'Yeah, but it's so boring,' said Prahati. 'Just dates and facts. What we need is something to spice up the project.'

'Like photos of the ruins or something?' Laila asked.

'Or find the secret passages,' Shalini added.

'Even finding Pia Ghosh there might help,' grinned Prahati.

Chapter 10

Laila sat at the dining table sorting through a large bunch of photographs. They were photos from her childhood, which Samir was coming over to look at, and maybe borrow a few for his project. Laila wanted to sift through them first and remove anything potentially embarrassing, even though she knew Murad was likely to have some compromising photos himself. She hoped Samir wouldn't think to ask him.

The dining room in their house was in the shorter arm of an L-shaped room. From her seat, she could just about see the TV and when she looked up, there was Sunil Saifi's face plastered all over it. The red blinking 'Breaking News' notice was flashing all over the screen. She got up and rushed closer to hear what was going on.

'...though it is unlikely. Our sources say that Sunil Saifi has fled to Australia, where he still has family, though people close to him are choosing to remain tight-lipped about his whereabouts. We have on the line former Indian captain and Saifi's mentor, Manjinder Singh. Sir, do you think he'll be present on the twentieth of October for his court date?'

But before Laila could hear what Manjinder Singh had to say, the door between the house and the shop swung open, and her mother's voice came through: 'Go right in. She's there.'

'Hi,' said Samir, stepping through.

Laila snapped off the TV. 'Hi. I have the photos ready.'

'Thanks.' Samir glanced towards the silent TV set. 'Did I just see Sunil Saifi's face?'

'Yeah, something about a court date.'

Samir stared at the blank screen. 'You really think he's a match-fixer?' he asked quietly.

'At first I didn't want to, but then,' Laila shrugged, 'he's confessed, so...'

'Yeah.' He stared at the floor and shuffled his feet. 'I used to think he was, I don't know...'

'I know.' Laila hesitated. 'I used to keep records—scorecards and all,' she said. 'I had a notebook. I even made wallpapers and collages.' She hadn't talked to any of her friends about the match-fixing scandal. Everyone knew that Saifi had been her hero. Laila thought they would laugh at her for idolizing a cheat and a match-fixer if the subject ever came up.

But Samir didn't laugh. He just nodded like it was the most normal thing. 'He was my favourite player. I feel it was all...I don't know...such a waste. You know what I mean?'

Laila did. They stared at each other for a few moments, mourning for their fallen hero.

When Laila turned up for cricket practice after school, one of the twins was by the bench at the edge of the field again, dressed in a grey tracksuit, nervously hopping from one foot to the other.

'Are you joining us?' Laila asked her. 'Davinder, is it?'

The girl smiled. 'Well done. Also, you can call me Davi.'

Laila grinned back. 'Just a guess. There's always fifty per cent chance of being right.'

'There's an easier way to tell us apart, actually.' She pointed to her ears.

Laila leaned forward. There were tiny silver earrings in the shape of the cursive letter 'd'.

'Sometimes even our parents can't tell us apart. So

they got us these.'

'How come nobody's ever noticed it?'

'Because unless you really look, the 'h' and the 'd' are sort of similar.'

'Well, thanks for telling me,' said Laila. 'Now tell me, are you really joining us? Aren't you in any other club?'

'I quit,' said Davi.

'To join cricket?'

She looked troubled. 'Ye-es...but...'

'Why's there a "but"? If you like it, join it.'

'No, you don't understand. I do like it. But my sister will never talk to me again.'

'What? Why?'

'We've always done everything together. Everything. Since the time we were babies. We even liked the same things. That's why we've been sent to boarding school. Our parents thought we would learn to mix and be independent of each other.'

'I still don't see why what's keeping you from joining us. That's being independent, right?'

'That's the thing. I've always liked what Harmi liked, even when I didn't like it.'

Laila was just about to say that that didn't make sense when she realized it did. 'You mean, you just pretended to like everything she did?'

Davi shrugged. 'It's not that straightforward. I do like most things she likes. We've always thought that we were no good at sports, but the thing is, I am. At least, I'm better than Harmi, and I like it. But I've never played anything seriously because I wanted to do things with her. But here, living with so many others... I just feel that sometimes I want to be a different person, not a photocopy.'

'Do you really think your sister will hate you because you're trying something you like?'

Davi thought for a moment. 'No, not when you put it like that.' She grinned suddenly. 'I think I'll give Cricket Club a try.'

'Hey, Photocopy, you joining us?' Anju called out as she passed by.

'The name's Davi,' Laila pointed out.

●

'What's wrong with Shalini?' Prahati whispered to Laila at assembly the next day.

'I was going to ask you that,' Laila whispered back.

Shalini was standing right at the end of the line, instead of her usual place with Laila and Prahati. Her eyes were red and swollen like she'd been crying, and her face was black as thunder.

The music teacher started playing the piano for the school song, and there was a discordant moment when everybody started singing at different times on different scales.

'I wish we could ask Jasmine,' Laila said, her gazed locked in front as they pretended to sing.

'Do you think it's Jasmine? Giving her a hard time about the project?'

'Really? That's a bit much, no?'

'Yeah, probably.'

'You know, some part of me really, *really* wants to know who lives in that house!'

'Is it because of the fancy new gates and CCTV or because of Jasmine?' asked Prahati, keeping an eye on Shabnam Miss, who was watching to see who wasn't singing.

'Well, probably the latter!'

The first period was second language, and Laila and Shalini both had Bengali. Laila decided that her duty as best friend was to at least try and talk to Shalini. And since asking her outright if something was wrong was not an option, she tried a different tactic.

She slipped into the seat next to Shalini and said in a low voice, 'Has Jasmine been troubling you about the project?'

'Jasmine what?' asked Shalini bewildered.

'You know what I mean. Since she was so weird to me about it.'

Shalini shook her head. 'She doesn't talk to me.'

'Oh.' Laila scratched her head—metaphorically—for something to say. She really hadn't thought it through.

'Actually, not threatening me about it might be her way of being nice to me,' said Shalini. 'Because I backed her when she took on Romi and Deepa, who were making some younger girls fetch and carry for them.'

It was Laila's turn to be surprised. About the news that Jasmine was standing up to the bullies as much about the fact that Shalini was suddenly talking normally.

'I really don't get her,' said Laila. 'She's moody and bad-tempered, but she can also be kind. She's so good with the younger girls during cricket. In fact, cricket is the only time she seems human.'

'Sometimes I feel that she's not really a bad person.' Shalini doodled on the corner of her notebook as she spoke. It was a dark, dense scribble, the pencil rubbing so hard on the paper that it tore. 'I think she's just sad about something and it comes out wrong.'

Laila had an uncomfortable feeling that she should read between the lines, but didn't know how to.

'We have to talk about our history project,' Prahati said a couple of days later when she and Laila were sitting on the lawn having their tiffin. 'The midterm break is coming in two weeks and Aunty wants ideas on format soon after.'

'For that we have to have a meeting,' Laila pointed out. 'All *three* of us.'

'You do it. She's your best friend.'

'But you see her more often.'

Whatever was going on with Shalini, she had decided to distance herself from her friends. Laila had tried a few times to talk to her, but she still preferred to be alone and finally Laila had given up.

'I bet everyone will either do a PowerPoint presentation or make a book,' said Prahati, licking tomato sauce from her tiffin box. 'We need to do something different.'

Laila felt gloomy. 'I bet Shalini would have an idea.'

'I think we need to forget about Shalini and figure this out ourselves.'

'It would be so great if we had some photos of the ruins.'

'We need to find a way of giving Phoolchand the slip,' said Prahati, 'and speak directly to the people living there.'

'Maybe Jasmine will put us in touch!' Just the thought made Laila laugh. She sighed a few moments later. 'This is not right, Shalini should be here.'

Chapter 11

'You know what you said about giving Phoolchand the slip yesterday?' Laila asked Prahati as they met outside the hostel to walk down to the school building. 'I might have an idea.'

'I'm not sure I want to know!'

Laila ignored that. 'I've been looking up the bill book at the shop and I noticed that every Friday afternoon Phoolchand comes by to drop their laundry and dry-cleaning, and collect the previous week's lot. So I could hang around near the house, and the moment Phoolchand leaves, I could pop over to the gate and talk to someone else and explain to them that we are not nosy journalists or anything, just kids.'

'But you're in school on Friday afternoons.'

'The midterm break is starting next Thursday. I could do it then.'

Prahati scrunched up her face, thinking. 'You know, that is quite a brilliant plan.'

'Thank you.'

'I have some news too. I'm not going away during the midterm break. My father has a work trip to Hong Kong and my mother decided to go with him. They'll be back for the parent–teacher conference, but it means I'll have to stay in the hostel. Maybe Aunty will give me a pass for Friday afternoon?'

'I know!' cried Laila. 'You could stay with me during the break. I'm sure my parents will say yes. Will you ask yours?'

But before Prahati could reply, the other boarders started coming in, with them Shalini.

Laila called out to her. She came over, but she wouldn't catch anyone's eye.

'We're making plans on how to get some photos of you-know-what,' said Prahati with a significant nod towards Jasmine who was arranging her pencil box on her desk. 'Are you staying in school during the break?'

'No,' said Shalini. 'But whatever you decide is fine with me.'

Hit for a Six

Samir was hugely excited to hear about their plan. 'Can I come?' he asked Laila the next time he was over, ostensibly to do more research for his project, but they just ended up chatting and playing with some stray puppies that were tottering about in the corner of their street.

'We're only going to ask for permission to explore the grounds,' said Laila.

'If you get to go inside, I mean.'

'I'll have to ask my friends.'

By the time the midterm break arrived, Laila and Prahati had their strategy ready. After lunch on Friday, they would go and hang around near the mouth of the lane and watch for Phoolchand to come sputtering up in his old scooter with the sidecar. They would see him coming in good time to hide. When it was safe, they would run down the lane to the house and use the intercom.

Friday arrived and Prahati and Laila were in a state of intense excitement. Samir called, asking if he and Murad could come over to play cricket, but Laila told him they were busy. Then they proceeded to irritate the life out of Laila's mother by hanging around the shop all morning, giddy with excitement.

'I know you're up to something,' her mother said. 'Please behave.'

However, everything went off without a hitch.

They hid behind trees, waiting for Phoolchand to pass, and then tore up the lane and pressed the bell on the intercom.

'Who's there?' a voice called out in Hindi.

'It's Phoolchand's wife!' hissed Prahati. 'She's never going to...'

Laila shushed her. 'We are students from Rosebud Academy,' she said, so politely that it hurt. 'We are doing a history project. We wanted to know if we could see the grounds.'

There was a silence. 'Rosebud Academy, did you say?' the voice asked finally, this time in English.

'Yes,' Prahati put in quickly, like the voice would go away if they didn't respond on time.

'Why do you want to see the grounds?'

Laila explained patiently again that the topic of their project was the house and that they would like to see the ruins in the grounds. 'We won't disturb you, ma'am,' she finished. 'Thought it would be great if you let us take some photos of the house too.'

'I see. How many of you?'

'There are three of us.'

'I see,' the voice said again. 'Why have you picked this house?'

'Er, our history teacher said we could pick any

colonial building in town,' said Prahati, leaning towards the intercom. 'So we chose this house because it has a long and interesting history.'

'Hmm, all right. Tell me your names and class.'

'Yesss!' Prahati whispered, with a fist pump, as Laila recited their names.

'Come back the Monday after next. Come in the morning, after nine.'

'But that's a school day, ma'am,' said Laila in dismay.

'I'm sorry,' the voice replied, quite reasonably. 'But it's the only time it will be possible.'

The girls exchanged glances, disappointed. Would Aunty allow them to miss school for a project?

•

The first day back after the midterm break was the parent–teacher conference. Laila was doing okay in school so she wasn't particularly worried, but decided it would be better to let her parents navigate the day themselves. Teachers and parents sometimes tended to send uncomfortable questions her way in each other's company.

She was drinking orange juice in the lawn when Prahati found her. 'Where have you been? I've been looking for you.'

'Avoiding my parents. Why?'

'It's about Shalini. She lied, she stayed in school during the break.'

'Why would she lie to us?'

'I don't know.'

Laila pressed her lips together, hurt that Shalini would lie to her.

There was a special assembly in the afternoon, to be followed by a grand tea to which all the parents were invited. Aunty, who always relished a chance to gush about the achievements of her students, was in her elements. Laila and Prahati spent their time playing noughts and crosses on a sheet of paper on their laps, but Aunty's final announcement made them look up.

'As you all know, the Rosebud Cricket Club has been training girls from the school and from the town for these past months. We were the first girls' cricket club in the district and even though it has been less than three months, two other clubs have started since. Seeing the enthusiastic response, a group of former cricketers have decided to hold a coaching camp next year. And I am delighted to announce that all our under-15 cricketers will all be eligible for selection.'

This time there were whoops and whistles, mostly from the girls, and especially the cricket-playing ones.

'For this, we must give a *big* hand to our wonderful cricket coach, former Test player and national coach, Ms S.M. Swapna, who has worked tirelessly to organize the camp.'

Swapna Miss was ushered to the mic amidst much applause. 'Credit goes to the girls,' she said. 'But first, we will have the cricket match. Chandnisarai versus Rosebud Academy at end of semester. I hope you will all come.'

●

While the girls were allowed to wander around and eat their mid-morning snacks wherever they wished, as a rule the whole school ate lunch together in the dining hall of the boarding house. A few days after the midterm break, during lunch, Shalini spilt dal on her T-shirt and went up to change. Laila decided it was time to bell the cat. She turned to Jasmine, who was sitting at their table.

'Hey,' she called. 'What's wrong with Shalini?'

Jasmine looked up, surprise writ large on her face. People generally didn't talk to her unless they had to. 'How should I know?'

'You're her roommate.'

'I'm not her minder. Ask her yourself.'

Prahati poked Laila. 'What are you doing?' she hissed.

'I need to know what's wrong with Shalini.'

Prahati stirred her dal. 'I'm sure if we were still roommates I'd have some idea what's up, but really, I don't.'

'Then you're not helping,' said Laila.

'Well don't bite my head off.'

'There are too many mysteries this semester.' Laila kept her voice low, glancing at Jasmine, who gave her a dirty look and got up with her plate. 'Sorry for snapping at you.'

'I know,' said Prahati gloomily. 'I wish Shalini would tell us what's going on.'

'Maybe she will when she can or when she wants to. But I'm not good at waiting for things to happen.'

'Poor Shalini. And with Miss Gloomy Gus as a roommate too. It must be a barrel of laughs in their room.'

Since their table was right by the edge of the door, they didn't see Shalini come in till it was too late.

'Thanks a lot,' she said, her voice shaking. 'I thought you were my friends. I was mistaken.' She turned and left.

Chapter 12

For a moment, Laila and Prahati were frozen to their seats. Then Laila pushed her chair away from the table so roughly that it toppled with a crash. She took off after Shalini.

'Hey!' Jasmine, doing her duty as a prefect, called out. A teacher called out as well, but Laila's feet were pounding down the corridor in pursuit of Shalini.

'Shalini, stop! You only heard part of the conversation!'

But Shalini didn't stop. She went up two flights of stairs and kept running. Laila followed doggedly. She knew she was going to be in trouble because day scholars were not allowed beyond the dining area, but she didn't care.

Shalini disappeared around a corner and two seconds later, when Laila turned the same corner, she bumped into her. But Shalini wasn't looking at Laila at all—in fact, she seemed to have all but forgotten that she'd been running. She was frowning, staring straight ahead at the doorway to the bathrooms.

Then Laila heard it. Quiet laughter intermingled with the sound of sobs.

Shalini started walking, fast, Laila after her. Inside the bathroom, they were met with the sight of Sheena and Romi, standing and giggling, while Tanvi and one of her classmates were kneeling, bent over their shoes with toothbrushes in their hands. The younger girls were sobbing.

'You've got to be kidding me!' Shalini said, teeth gritted.

Everyone jumped. Romi was about to say something, but Shalini walked right up to her, in her face. She bunched Romi's T-shirt in her fist and pushed her hard against the wall. There was a dull thump as Romi's head made contact with the wall behind her.

'I've had enough of you thugs!' shouted Shalini. 'Ragging is a criminal offence. I'm going to lodge an FIR and send you to jail! Where you belong!'

Romi's eyes went round with fear.

'Shalini!'

Laila turned around and found Gayathri Miss,

Vinod Sir, Prahati, Jasmine and a few other girls crowding into the bathroom area.

'What is the meaning of this behaviour, Shalini?' Gayathri Miss's voice was raised in anger.

'No, no, Miss, it's not her,' Laila began urgently, but she needn't have bothered.

Sheena was cowering against the wall, next to Romi, crying. 'Sorry, Miss. It was just a joke, we didn't mean any harm.'

'Yes, Miss, just a joke,' Romi sobbed. 'Please don't call the police. My parents will kill me. Just harmless fun.'

'You should ask the younger girls how much fun and exactly how harmless,' another boarder called out from the back of the crowd.

There were murmurs of agreement.

'They've been bullying the juniors since day one, Miss,' someone else said.

Tanvi and her friend were standing with their heads lowered, holding their toothbrushes guiltily, like they were the ones caught doing something wrong. Laila nudged her. 'Say something.'

'Y...yes, Miss,' the younger girl muttered.

'You mean to say all this has been going on for two months and not one of you has said *anything*?' thundered Gayathri Miss.

There was silence, except for the bullies' sobs.

'Leave now, the rest of you,' said Gayathri Miss. 'Any day scholars found lingering in the hostel will be severely punished. Now!'

They filed out, and Laila found herself surrounded by students wanting to know what had happened.

•

Romi, Sheena and Deepa were expelled, and the school remained in shock for the next few days. This was a first for Rosebud Academy.

'There was huge drama last evening,' Shilpa reported to Laila and the other day scholars the next day. 'They were told to pack and were moved out of the hostel into the guest house. Then, in the evening Romi and Deepa's parents turned up, and Sheena's came this morning.'

There was a special assembly and Aunty spoke at length about bullying and how there was no place in Rosebud for those who made anyone uncomfortable. Shalini was quite a hero among the students, but she didn't seem to be any happier for it.

'Is it true, can you be sent to jail for ragging?' Laila asked her.

She shrugged. 'No idea. I just said the first thing that came to my mind.'

'Well, it was quick thinking. I am impressed.'

Shalini nodded and turned to go. Laila caught her arm. 'What you heard yesterday in the dining hall, that was only part of the conversation.'

'You were making fun of me.' Shalini's voice was hard.

'We weren't. I promise.'

Shalini held Laila's gaze. Her lips were pressed so hard together, they were a thin line. Then she said, 'My parents are getting divorced.'

Laila's mouth fell open. She shut it quickly, then opened it to say something. But she didn't know what to say. Divorced?

In the eight or so years of their friendship, Laila had only met Shalini's parents about three times. She caught herself wondering why the divorce made any difference to Shalini since they were hardly around anyway. But of course, it's not the kind of thing you can wonder aloud.

'But...then why did you move away to stay with them?' Laila stammered out.

Shalini's shoulders rose and fell in a shrug. 'My aunt says she can't look after me any more.'

'So, then...what will happen?'

Shalini shrugged again.

'Why didn't you tell us?'

'And then what? So you all, with your normal families,

can laugh at me, feel sorry for me? You think I like this? Not being wanted? Listening to my aunt complaining all the time how hard it is to take care of a teenage girl and my parents fighting over who should get to keep me, like I'm a *thing*?'

Laila was silent. How come she had never realized that Shalini was unhappy? She swallowed and then pointed to her own face. 'Does it look like I'm laughing?'

'But you do feel sorry for me.'

'I feel angry for you.'

Shalini sighed. She looked away. 'I don't want anyone to know.'

'Okay.' Then Laila added hesitantly, 'But it's not hard to figure out that something's wrong.'

Shalini closed her eyes for a moment. 'Fine, I'll try to be more normal.'

Laila didn't see why she had to. Didn't you have a right to be angry, to be upset, to show your feelings? 'Why should you?' she said. 'Let people think whatever. We'll deal with them.' She pushed up the sleeves of her T-shirt threateningly.

Shalini smiled and rolled her eyes.

●

'We should do a website,' said Shalini. 'For our project.'

'How are we going to manage that?' Prahati asked.

'We're learning how to make websites in Computer Club. I think I can do it. Gayathri Miss will definitely help me. Professor Pradhan said he could give us some images.'

'Plus, we have our meeting at Old Mister Marshall's place on Monday,' Laila pointed out. 'Let's hope they let us take photos.'

Aunty was surprisingly amenable to them missing half a day of school. 'You must think for yourselves,' she said when they went to ask her for permission. 'If you feel you must sacrifice half a day of schoolwork to get your project done, that is something you will just have to manage.'

'Did she say yes or was she being sarcastic?' Laila asked, somewhat confused after they left her office.

'I'm pretty sure that was a straightforward yes,' said Prahati.

'Should we take a gift?' asked Shalini, who was back to being more or less normal with them, which was a relief. If Prahati was surprised, she didn't show it. It still bothered Laila, though, that she couldn't do anything to help Shalini.

'Why?' asked Laila.

'It's nice to take a gift when you go to someone's house.'

'It's not a birthday party,' said Prahati.

'We didn't take one for Professor Pradhan,' Laila pointed out.

'Just a thought.'

Chapter 13

When they met at Laila's place on Monday morning, she showed them a small, painted clay jar that she'd put inside a cardboard box.

'I made it during that pottery workshop we had,' she said. 'I thought it'd make a nice gift.'

They trotted up the lane, somewhat nervous. Prahati had a digital camera with her.

'I saw the silver Honda City going down the main road this morning,' Laila told the others. 'I hope they haven't forgotten our appointment.'

They pressed the bell and for a long time nothing happened. Then, with a loud clang, the metal door set into the gigantic gates opened and Phoolchand scowled at them.

They followed him silently up the driveway that curved between the neat lawns. Two gardeners were at work, one mowing the grass, the other tending a flowerbed. The front door opened just as they reached it and the woman that Laila had seen on the day they arrived stepped outside.

'Good morning,' she said.

'Good morning, ma'am,' the girls chorused.

'You can call me Saira.' She had a slight lilt to her voice, a hint of an accent. 'Now tell me, which one of you is which.'

They introduced themselves. 'Thank you for letting us come,' said Laila in her deathly polite voice. 'We brought you a gift.' She proffered the box, enclosed in a brown paper bag.

Saira opened it immediately. 'Oh how lovely, thank you. Did you make it?'

Laila nodded.

Saira led the way towards the back of the house. Flowerbeds ran all the way around and there were more lawns. There was a badminton court and also a rolled-up matting wicket inside a net.

'Do you play cricket?' Prahati asked incongruously.

Saira laughed. 'No, but my children do.'

'Do you have a swimming pool in the house?' Laila

asked. Local rumour had it that there was an indoor pool.

'I wish we did, but no.' Then she added, with a twinkle in her eye: 'And before you ask, nor do we have any Bollywood stars in the house.'

The girls smiled politely.

Saira seemed quite normal, veering towards the nice and friendly end of the scale. Why would someone like that choose to live in such secrecy, wondered Laila.

She also seemed to know her way around the grounds and its history. She led them past the back lawns, into the forest, which was part of the property, and where the ruins were.

'Wow,' said Prahati, looking around at the crumbling walls, with plants growing through the cracks. 'Is this really part of the old inn?'

Saira confirmed that it was.

'You've made the rest of the house so nice,' said Shalini, 'but how come you've left these ruins just as they are? Don't you want to demolish them and make something nice?'

'Oh no, I don't think so!' Saira seemed quite shocked at the suggestion. 'How could I destroy all that history? In fact, I want to find out if there's a way to restore this place—at least superficially.'

'Do you know about the secret passages?' Laila asked.

'Of course. But they've long since been blocked off.'

That was disappointing. 'Are you sure?'

Saira smiled. 'Quite. I checked and double-checked myself. It would have been a nightmare if anyone from the forest could just stroll into the house.'

She had a point. It was a pity, though, as Laila had had dreams of finding a secret passage.

'I can show you where they were, though, at least the one from the grounds to the forest,' said Saira. She led them through the trees, emerging out into a small clearing. There was a platform that looked very close to falling to pieces, with a circular opening on it's surface that was now bricked up pretty thoroughly. 'That was the well,' she said. 'The passage starts inside it. It comes out about two kilometres into the forest, very close to the river.'

'Inside the well?' Prahati asked. 'How did people get in and out?'

'There were hand and foot holds cut inside the well shaft. I imagine it was pretty dangerous, but the people who wanted to escape must have been desperate.'

'Can we take photos?' Laila asked.

Saira nodded, and Prahati got to work with her camera.

'We've heard there were other passages,' said Shalini.

'One from the cellars,' Saira replied, 'and there are conflicting reports of where it led. Some people say it went into the forest and others say it led to the court house.'

'Is that sealed too?'

'Very much so.'

The girls looked at each other, somewhat disappointed.

'I'll show you something interesting, though,' Saira offered. She took them around the crumbling edifice of what might once have been a room. She pointed at the bottom, where the undergrowth had been cleared away. 'See here, you can see two kinds of brickwork. So this lower part must be from the original caravanserai, and the upper portions from when it was repaired and rebuilt later.'

It turned out that Saira knew a fair bit of the history of the area and also about historical architecture. She showed them the different kind of bricks they used back then and also had a fair bit to add about what the layout of the inn might have been like.

She waited while the girls took photos and then she invited them back to the house for a snack. 'Are you interested in the house itself?' she asked. 'It is an interesting mix of architectural styles.'

Of course, they were only too keen. So Saira pointed out various elements, as Laila and Shalini made notes and Prahati took photographs.

'You know a lot about the place,' Laila observed.

'I used to be a history teacher,' said Saira. 'I do miss teaching.'

'Why did you stop?' Prahati asked.

'My health isn't what it used to be.'

Inside, the girls stared in awe at the high ceilings, the old-fashioned light fittings with modern LED bulbs, the long-stemmed fans and a great deal of heavy, old-style furniture.

'Is this furniture from olden times?' Shalini asked.

'Some of it is, but mostly they are copies,' said Saira. 'Some items have been salvaged and repaired.' She patted a dark and heavy wooden cabinet with glass-fronted panels. 'This one is a survivor, though. We had to do some minor repairs, but it dates back to more than a hundred years. See that manufacturer's plaque there? That's the original.'

There were various knick-knacks inside, mostly handicrafts. Saira set down the pot that Laila had made on top of the cabinet, next to an ornate candleholder.

'Could we take a photo of the cabinet?' Prahati asked.

'Sure,' said Saira.

A young woman came in shortly, wheeling a trolley, ensconced in a delicious smell of pakodas. Saira bade them sit and served out tea and snacks. As they ate and drank, she asked them questions about their school.

'Do any of you play cricket?' she asked.

'We do.' Laila pointed to Prahati and herself. 'We're going to have a match against the town girls in December.'

Saira smiled. 'So I heard. That's very good news. Do you want some more tea?'

They declined, but Saira excused herself to get some more.

'She's nice,' Prahati whispered when she was gone. 'Why does she want to hide inside here?'

'Well, if you had to hide somewhere,' said Laila, 'what could be more fantastic than this place?'

'Plus, she said something about health,' Shalini added. 'Maybe she's sick?'

'Hey, how did she know about the cricket match?' Prahati asked.

Laila shrugged. 'Local gossip?'

'But she never goes out anywhere.'

Saira came back into the room, so they couldn't speculate any more. Just as she sat down, a low phone ringtone sounded.

'Oh, excuse me, I have to get that.' Saira bent over to pick up her mobile phone, which had been lying face down on a side table. She took a look at the screen before answering. 'Hello?' She listened with a small frown on her face. 'Oh. Do you know when?' Pause. 'I see. Are you on your way back?' Another pause. 'That was fast...' She nodded as the person on the other end spoke. 'I see. Just as well you didn't have to go all the way. All right. See you soon.'

She disconnected the phone and looked at the girls apologetically. 'Sorry to be so rude, but you'll have to leave soon.'

'It's okay,' said Prahati. 'We need to be back at school before lunch.'

'Thank you, ma'am...Saira,' Laila said, standing up. 'You've been very helpful and generous.'

'You're very welcome. This was great fun for me too. I hope you will come again.' She looked troubled for a moment. 'Though I'm not sure when.'

They got up to leave. 'I have one last question,' Prahati said. 'Did you buy this house from the Taleem Foundation?'

'Oh, no, it still belongs to them.'

Laila trailed behind the others as they walked out to the hall. She leaned forward to examine the old cabinet once again. Something caught her eye—a metal disk, like a large coin, maybe a little smaller than her palm, with some sort of complicated logo on it of two grey birds hanging on to a green-and-gold shield. There was a golden crown, with a staff on top, plus some leaves and flowers set in a flowing sort of design. The thing looked old and had a deep notch on the top. There was lettering at the bottom too, but the others were almost out of the door, so she had to run.

Where had she seen that design before, Laila wondered.

Chapter 14

'Miss, how can I search for an image online?' asked Laila, scrolling down a screenful of useless images.

'What sort of image?' Gayathri Miss asked.

'I'm looking for a logo or a crest—I don't know what you call them.'

'A coat of arms?'

'Right, that's it.' She changed the search term from 'logo with birds, shield, crown and staff' to 'coat of arms with birds, shield, crown and staff' and pressed Enter.

'There you go,' said Gayathri Miss.

Laila ran her eyes down the screen tiled with coats of arms of various kinds. She scrolled the page. 'The one I want is not here.'

'What about this one—it has birds, a shield and a crown?'

She shook her head. 'No. The one I'm looking for had something written too.'

'Do you remember the words.'

'No.'

'Keep scrolling, you might still find it. But if you could recall the words, that might help.'

When the bell rang, signalling the end of the lunch break, Laila still hadn't found what she was looking for.

●

Prahati had been partly right about the PowerPoint presentations and books, though they were not the only team with an innovative idea. The Glen Hotel group had decided to do a book because they had collected dozens of old photographs of the hotel over the past century or so. The Parsi Colony group were doing a PowerPoint presentation. They had lots of digital photos and had done an admirable number of interviews. But the most interesting idea, Laila willingly admitted, was Jasmine's group, who were doing the Mall Road.

'We're doing a panorama,' said Davi, who was presenting on behalf of the group. 'We're going to take pictures of the entire Mall Road and put them up in sequence to recreate the stretch. Then we're going to do a short write-up on each relevant building or landmark.'

'Lovely,' said Aunty, beaming. 'But printing photos is expensive. I want to see a budget, and I want to know how you're going to fund it. By the end of next week, please.'

Prahati got up to talk about her group. 'We'll be doing a website, Miss,' she said. 'We have photographs, plus some images that Professor Pradhan has promised to give us. The house has a long history, and we thought we could try and focus on the architecture and how it changed over the last century. If we find more information later, we can add it to the website.'

Aunty looked like she approved. 'Interesting. Did you have a fruitful interview at the house?'

'Yes, Miss. It was very illuminating.'

'You *went* to the house?' Sanya asked during break. 'That's where you were yesterday! So, spill the beans, who lives there?'

From the corner of her eye, Laila could see Jasmine hovering at the door of the classroom, her expression murderous.

'No Bollywood stars,' said Laila.

'Are you sure?'

'Quite.'

'Then who?'

'Just normal people.' Laila was getting tired of Sanya's questions and Jasmine throwing visual daggers at her. 'Who don't want nosy people like you wanting to know what time they go to the toilet.'

She picked up her tiffin and brushed past Sanya and Jasmine. She might have imagined it, but Jasmine looked rather relieved.

●

Laila lay on the grass copying Davi's science notes from the class they had missed when they had gone to see Saira at the house. She listened with half a ear to the others talking about the cricket match-fixing scandal, which was back in the news these days, because the court hearing had been postponed for the second time.

'My father says they're all going to get off,' Prahati said. 'He said the next time somebody's grandma is going to die.'

Laila felt she had to jump in. 'It's hardly his fault his dad died that morning.'

'How can they get off if they've confessed?' Shalini wanted to know.

'Only Sunil Saifi and Prashanth Kaushik have

confessed,' Laila pointed, sitting up and shutting her notebook.

'These lawyers, they'll find a way,' said Prahati darkly.

'So when is the next date?' Shalini asked.

'In January,' Laila replied. 'Have you guys read that really funny piece G. Sharda did in *India Today*?'

Prahati laughed. 'Yeah, I saw it in the library. That part about going to bed clutching their lucky teddies was hilarious.'

'What have teddy bears got to do with it?' Shalini asked, puzzled.

'Oho, she was making fun of them.'

'Lucky charms,' said Laila to no one in particular.

'What?' asked Shalini.

'Nothing...' Only, it wasn't nothing. It rang a bell, a loud one. 'Hey, what was the date when we went to the house?'

'It was the day before yesterday,' said Prahati, 'Monday.'

'I know it was Monday. What was the date?'

'Twentieth. Why?' said Prahati.

Laila didn't answer. In fact, she didn't talk much for the rest of the day.

Laila was thoroughly distracted at cricket that afternoon.

So much so that she spent most of her time taking punishment rounds of the field. During fielding practice, she repeatedly let the ball slip through her legs, and also got her little finger trapped between the ball and the ground while doing close-in catching drills. During her batting stint, she only managed to make contact with three balls, one of which she lobbed back to Tara for an easy catch. Swapna Miss was disgusted with her.

'You are not behaving like an opener,' she admonished her after the caught-and-bowled incident, 'you are behaving like number eleven! Waving bat like that as if you are the Mahinder Singh Dhoni at 20-20 World Cup final! You are standing in front of wicket but in the mind you are gone somewhere else! Chandnisarai girls will laugh at you, laugh at whole team if you play like this. You want that? You tell me, you want that?'

'No, Miss,' said Laila miserably. 'Sorry.'

'You will be more sorry after you take the five rounds. Go now!'

She was ready to drop by the time she got home, but she had more important things to check. Without even bothering to wash her hands or get something to eat, she switched on the computer and accessed the Dropbox account they were using to store their research for the project.

Prahati had uploaded all the photos there, and Laila scrolled through them until she found the ones of the cabinet. There were three—one had the whole cabinet in the frame and the other two were close-ups of the maker's plaque, screwed into the wood just above the point where the doors of the cabinet closed. It was the latter two that interested Laila.

In one of them, the flash had reflected off the glass and you couldn't see anything inside. But after that Prahati must have turned off the flash, for in the other one, not only was the manufacturer's disc clearly in focus, some of the items on the top shelf were visible as well. And it included that strange, large coin-like thing that had been poking Laila's brain for days.

Luckily, Prahati had a steady hand and even through the glass, Laila could make out some lettering on the logo. She zoomed as much as she could into the image without getting it pixellated. Even so, because of the glass, it wasn't very clear, but eventually Laila pieced together what it said: 'Forward in faith'.

Then, she opened a new tab on the browser and typed the phrase in, within quotes, followed by 'coat of arms with birds, shield and crown'.

The first search result said, 'City of Wagga Wagga (NSW, Australia)'. But Laila didn't click through. She didn't need to. She knew why that coin-like thing had been bothering her.

She went up the narrow staircase at the back of the house, up into the storeroom. A few minutes later, she came staggering back down with a cardboard box full of magazines. She knew what she was looking for and if she found it, it would be a corroboration of her theory.

Not that she needed it. She had a pretty good idea who was living in SJ House. If she was right, it also made sense why they were so secretive.

Chapter 15

Laila hung around the hostel, hiding behind a tree so Shalini or Prahati wouldn't see her first. The person she was hoping to catch was Jasmine. Luckily, she spotted her soon, walking across the quadrangle.

Looking around to see that her friends were around, Laila ran up to Jasmine. 'Hey, I need to talk to you.'

'Why?' demanded Jasmine.

'It's about the house!' Laila turned and started to walk away, fast, away from the hostel and school building, knowing Jasmine would follow.

Sure enough, Jasmine ran after her and grabbed her shoulder. 'What?'

Laila shrugged off her hand. 'First, don't touch me.'

She turned again and continued walking till they were behind the sports shed. There was an old concrete bench there that no one used much except the birds. Finally, she turned around and faced Jasmine. 'You know who lives there, right?'

Jasmine crossed her arms across her chest. 'What if I do?'

'Jasmine!' Laila wanted to shake her. 'It's Sunil Saifi, the cricketer! Or former cricketer, I should...ah!'

Jasmine had shoved her back against the shed, pinning her to the wall. 'You...! Who have you told?'

Laila pushed her hand away. 'I haven't told anyone. What's wrong with you? I'm telling *you*, because I'm guessing you already know, though I have no idea how or why. I had to tell *some*one. I was going to go crazy!'

Jasmine deflated visibly. She sat down on ground, her back against the bench. 'How did you find out?' she asked in a flat voice.

'I guessed,' Laila replied. 'I knew about that lucky talisman he had when he had just got selected for India, even about the chip on the edge. There was a feature on him in a magazine a few years ago and they had a photo of it. Then, the other day, when we went to the house, I saw it there in a cabinet. At that time I thought it looked familiar but I didn't realize what it was. There were also cricket nets in the house, and his mother—at least I think that was his mother—said her kids played.

'Finally, and what made me sure was that we were asked to come on a particular day. It was the twentieth of October, the day of the court hearing, so he wouldn't be home and it would be safe for us to go. But Prashanth Kaushik's father died suddenly that morning and the hearing was postponed. Saira got a call while we were there and told us we had to leave right away. At that time I didn't realize what it meant, but I think that's what the call was about, to say he was on his way back.'

Jasmine exhaled loudly. 'Wow.'

Laila sat down beside her. 'How come *you* knew?'

'Because he's my brother.'

'*What!*'

Jasmine nodded slowly. She looked up at the sky and closed her eyes. 'That freaking idiot Sunil Saifi is my brother.' Only, she didn't say 'freaking' but another word that would mean immediate suspension if any of the teachers heard it. 'Hell, I haven't said that aloud for goodness knows how long.'

'But...*how*? Your names...'

'He's always used our mother's surname.'

'But he's waaaay older than you.'

'What's wrong with you? I'm telling you that the guy who took money to throw matches is my brother and you keep contradicting me! And yes, he's sixteen years older than me. It happens.'

'Wow.' It was Laila's turn to say that. 'Is that why you've been such a super-grouch? Because your brother is a national-hero-turned-national-villain?'

'That and because I had to leave Australia and move to India with my mother just when I was a shoo-in for the under-15 state team. And mostly because after all this rubbish with idiot Sunil, my mother had a heart attack.'

'Shit!' said Laila before she could stop herself.

Jasmine hugged her knees and rested her forehead on them. 'Yeah.'

'Is she okay now?'

Jasmine nodded. 'She is, but I'm worried about her.'

'So you grew up in Australia? That's why you have a weird accent?'

'What? I don't have a weird accent. *You* all have weird accents!'

'Why did you move to India?'

'My mother had been wanting to come back. She wanted to be more closely involved with...' She paused and looked at Laila. 'Can I tell you another secret?'

'There's more? Sure!'

'Have you heard of the Taleem Foundation?'

'Yeah. It's that NGO or trust or whatever that owns Old Mister Marshall's house?'

'Yep. So Taleem Foundation was started by my mother. Sunil has also worked really hard for it, idiot that he is otherwise. They raise funds for rural schools, and Mum has been wanting to start her own school, especially one that has a strong sports programme for girls. But she was never able to—said the timing wasn't right. When she heard of Rosebud Academy, she decided to donate money to it instead.'

'Whoa! *Your* family is the anonymous donor?'

'The Taleem Foundation actually.'

'Wow,' said Laila yet again, because that seemed to be the only apt response.

'Please don't tell anyone.'

'It's not my secret to tell.'

'But what about your project?'

'Our project is the history of the house, not who lives in it right now.'

'So you won't tell your friends?'

Leela was torn. Samir, for one, would definitely be interested. 'I guess I have no reason to.'

'I'm sorry I chucked a wobbly back then about your project. I was so afraid you'd find out.'

'No problem,' said Laila. 'I'm guessing chucked a wobbly means you lost your mind and behaved like an ass. Hey, if your family stays in town, why are you in the hostel?'

She shrugged. 'To maintain the secrecy. Also, I'm not talking to Sunil. Scum!'

Laila studied her. What would it be like if Zainab became really famous, like a household name around the world, and then she did something really terrible that made everyone hate her? Sunil Saifi had even had stones and shoes thrown at him a couple of times when he had appeared in public.

'He was my hero.' Laila clasped her hands between her knees.

'I'm sorry,' said Jasmine.

'Why? It's not your fault.' She looked at Jasmine. 'You know, you two are freakishly similar to look at. Even your batting styles are similar. But I would have never guessed you were related if you hadn't told me.'

'Thanks for not telling anyone.'

'Sure,' said Laila. She sighed. 'I'm sorry about your mother. I hope she stays well.'

'Thanks,' Jasmine replied in a small voice. 'I hope so too.'

If she were Prahati, thought Laila, she'd have hugged

Jasmine. Laila herself wasn't the touchy-feely type, though.

'I really don't get people sometimes,' she said instead. 'Having friends is not a bad thing. Why have you been moping all alone? You and Shalini both. Yours must be the funnest room in the hostel!'

'What's Shalini moping about?'

'If you two just talked to each other, you'd know.'

Jasmine sighed loudly. 'It's not like I can talk if I wanted to. Like you said, other people's secrets. If I tell that I'm related to Sunil or my mother lives in the house, it would get complicated.'

Laila sighed too. 'Yeah, you're right.' She shook her head. 'Grown-ups can make life so complicated for us, no?'

'Tell me about it.'

'Well, at least now I know why you're so good at cricket.'

'I'm not that good,' said Jasmine modestly. 'Just that I've been playing since I was five. It's just so frustrating there's no set-up here.'

'At least we've started something,' Laila pointed out, a tad defensive.

'True.'

'The projector is not working!'

'Have you turned on the power button?'

'*Yes!*'

'Okay, sorry! Check the connections.'

The classroom was in mayhem. It was Parents' Day the next day and they only had that morning to set up their projects to display to the parents. Each group had been given their own space in the classroom, but even so, everyone was getting in each other's way. Tempers were a bit frayed too.

'Does this plug go here or here?' called Laila from the under the table, where she had crawled to set up the PC they had lugged from the computer room to set up their project on.

Shalini crawled in next to her to help. 'The classroom is such a mess,' she said. 'Do you think we'll be able to get everything ready in time?'

'Harmi! Get off the chair! You're standing on the photos!' someone screamed.

'No, you're not doing it right!' someone else argued.

'Shut up or do it yourself!'

'It'll be a miracle,' said Laila, crossing her fingers and jamming the plug in. 'Ow, stop pushing me.'

'I'm not pushing! There's no space here.'

There was the sound of running feet and a breathless

voice called out: 'The cricket uniforms are here!'

Laila banged her head against the underneath of the table in her excitement to get out. 'See you in a bit,' she called to Shalini, as she and Prahati took off after Tara, the messenger.

'Hey, what's the meaning of this, leaving me all alone!' cried Shalini, but Laila kept running.

Not only had the cricket uniforms arrived—white T-shirts with the Rosebud Academy crest and white trousers—but Swapna Miss had also put up the final XI for the match against Chandnisarai Girls the next day.

Jasmine was captain, no surprises, with Anju as vice-captain. Nilofer and Laila were opening the batting. Prahati and Shilpi were both in, and so was Rukmini as wicketkeeper. Tara was the only class seven girl who had made it. The other three were from class nine. Davi was thrilled to be named twelfth man ('Twelfth woman,' she insisted).

'Is your mother coming?' Laila asked Jasmine when they were trying out their kit.

'Yes, I managed to convince her.'

'My pants are too long!' wailed Tara.

'Don't worry, we'll take a stapler to it tonight,' Jasmine told her.

'Something's changed with Jasmine these last couple

of weeks, no?' Prahati said when they were going back to their classroom to finish setting up the history exhibition.

Laila smiled to herself. 'Yep.'

Chapter 16

The day of the match, and the exhibition, was a cold and sunny December morning. There was quite a crowd at the Chandnisarai Sports Club grounds—most of the parents had turned up, as had many people from the town, especially those whose daughters were playing. Laila spotted Samir and Murad, and some of their friends, sitting cross-legged on the ground. They waved to her. 'All the best!' Samir yelled. Of course, all the students and teachers from Rosebud Academy were there.

The Chandnisarai girls seemed to be much bigger and stronger than the Rosebud cricketers. Laila eyed them in dismay as the captains went for the toss.

'We're batting,' Jasmine announced when she came back.

'They're going to cream us,' Laila said to her as they warmed up.

'Go in with that attitude and they will,' Jasmine admonished. 'They might look stronger, but I bet we can run faster. So we'll make more runs.'

Swapna Miss came to talk to them as they congregated in a huddle. She looked rather pleased. 'I have the surprise for you. Remember I told you about camp? Selectors are here. So you play two hundred per cent, okay?'

There was a murmur of assent.

'OKAY?' roared Swapna Miss, making them all jump.

'YES, MISS!' cried all twelve of them.

●

Laila was trembling equally with excitement and nerves as she walked out to open the batting. The Chandnisarai girls were spread out in their fielding positions and a tall girl who looked like she was at least eighteen was marking out her bowling run-up.

'Good luck,' said Nilofer as they parted ways. Laila wasn't facing, which was a minor relief.

The umpire called play and the bowler tore in for the first ball. Laila's heart was thumping, but the first ball was a bit short. Nilofer rocked on to her back foot and smashed it fine towards third man. The boundary was short on that side and before the long-stop fielder could get to it, it had crossed the boundary. The crowd cheered, while the Chandnisarai captain said some bad words to the bowler that made Laila grin.

Nilofer played the next ball through cover for a single, and it was Laila's turn to face the bowling. She took guard, her heart again in overdrive. But once the bowler started running in, Laila focused on the ball and forgot about everything else. All she saw was the red ball, bobbing as the bowler's arms pumped up and down. She leapt, her arm went around and up, and the ball was released. It flew true and straight down the pitch, hit the matting on the edge of the seam and cut slightly in. Laila brought her bat and pad together to defend and felt the satisfying thud of the ball hitting the thickest part of the bat. There was enough momentum to make the ball scurry back along the mat to the bowler, who bent to pick it up, but missed.

The umpire jumped out of the way as it rolled past the wickets at the non-striker's end.

'Yes!' screamed Laila, already halfway down the pitch. 'Yes, yes, yes!'

Nilofer didn't need much convincing and they were both safely home.

Laila felt the tension easing now that she had opened her account. It helped that the next delivery was a no-ball. Nilofer heard it early and smacked it as hard as she could. It didn't go far, but the fielder fumbled and they took another single. The next two balls were dots, and Laila played the final delivery of the over straight down the ground for two runs. Ten in the first over. Not bad.

The Chandnisarai captain brought an off-spinner on at the other end. It was a bit unusual, but Laila suspected that she was probably their secret weapon. She was right. Watching from the non-striker's end, she saw the ball pitching and turning sharply. Nilofer defended, but the ball thudded into her pads. The Chandnisarai team went up in a howl of appeal, but it had clearly been too high and the umpire shook his head gravely. The next ball didn't turn as much, and Nilofer pushed it to midwicket for a run.

The first ball Laila faced from the spinner also turned crazily, but she went down on one knee and swept it. It zipped to the fielder too quickly for them to risk a run. Nilofer and Laila had a short conference at the middle of the pitch and decided to be very careful about the spinner.

Whether it was the waywardness of their opening bowler that had made them jittery or whether they were just not well prepared, the Chandnisarai bowlers were a bit all over the place. Their fielding, though, was very good, and the wicketkeeper was excellent, as Nilofer found out some time later when she attempted to come down the wicket to a left-arm spinner, missed and was stumped.

With only five more runs added to the board, Shivi, the number three, was run out after a silly mix-up. Laila was relieved to see Jasmine coming out at her usual number four. The bowling was cattle fodder for Jasmine, who toyed with it at will. Laila only focused on giving the strike back to her, and they put on a seventy-three-run partnership of which Jasmine made fifty-five.

Jasmine was caught at mid-off in the twenty-second over. The score was a hundred and two. With just three more overs to go, Rakhi, ordinarily supposed to come in at number nine, was promoted up the order. Rakhi was the biggest of the Rosebud players and while Swapna Miss despaired at her batting technique, she was the only one apart from Jasmine capable of sending the ball out of the—smallish—ground. And she did manage a six, but was caught behind—the wicketkeeper taking a fantastic low catch—the very next ball.

Rosebud finished at a 113 for five. Laila was caught on the last ball trying to smash it as hard as she could. It ballooned up and the wicketkeeper took an easy catch. She had made thirty-two, nothing great, but Swapna Miss patted her on the back and said she had 'done the great job of holding innings together'.

●

At first, everything went Rosebud's way. The Chandnisarai opener was clean bowled in the very first over with no runs on the board when she tried to get out of the way of Shilpi's yorker. In the next over, Rakhi appealed for an LBW and got it. In the third over, the number three edged Shilpi comfortably into Rukmini's gloves.

Rosebud went mad with joy. They hugged each other and danced around Shilpi as the batter made her way forlornly back to the benches. Samir, Murad and their band of friends went quite nuts too. Only Swapna Miss was circumspect.

'Match is not over!' she shouted from the boundary. She sent Davi in with a bottle of water as an excuse to carry a message.

'Miss says that you should watch out for their next batter, Yamini,' she said quietly to the huddle of Rosebud cricketers.

But Rakhi bowled a somewhat wayward over next and Swapna Miss's prediction came true. Yamini creamed her around the ground, taking a full twenty runs off those six balls. Five of those came from a wide that Rukmini misjudged and edged it to the boundary. Even though twenty-five for three wasn't a fantastic score, it was much better than the five for three it had been not too long ago.

Jasmine brought herself on, but Yamini comfortably tucked her all around the ground for easy singles and twos. Prahati, generally a tight medium-pacer, also couldn't find her line and length, and the fielding started to show holes. Anju dropped a simple catch at slip, Rukmini missed a stumping and Shilpi overran the ball at the boundary. After ten overs, the score rose to fifty-nine, with no further loss, with the credit equally shared by Yamini and the shoddy fielding.

At the drinks break after twelve overs, Jasmine gathered the team around. 'We've gone and lost our advantage, and they've got a steady rhythm. If we don't break this partnership, we're definitely losing this match.'

'What do we do?' Anju asked. 'We need a plan?'

'I have a plan.' said Jasmine. She told them what it was and everyone went back to their fielding positions.

Laila, patrolling the cover boundary, chewed her nails anxiously as Shilpi marked her run-up again. This could be risky.

The Chandnisarai pair looked surprised to see Shilpi back. They were even more surprised to find fielders closing in around the striker. They met for a mid-pitch conference. Yamini said something and the other girl nodded, going back to take strike. Shilpi's first delivery was driven along the ground towards Laila, who picked it up easily and threw it back to Rukmini.

Yamini was now on strike. Shilpi ran in and bowled. It was defended. Jasmine picked it up at gully. No run. In the next ball, Laila knew from the way Yamini played her shot that she had been trying to lift the ball over the in-fielders but had been a fraction early. Actually, it wasn't the shot that was at fault—Shilpi had bowled a slower delivery that Yamini had misjudged. The ball flew up into the air on the offside. Jasmine called it and took an easy catch. The plan had worked.

The middle order collapsed in a heap after Yamini's departure, but Chandnisarai's tail proved that it had a sting. Parveen, the befuddling spinner who had opened their bowling, came in at number ten and threw her bat around in cavalier fashion. She probably had a guardian angel on call because all her mistimed shots fell safely between fielders, and she even managed a couple of boundaries. After twenty-one overs, the score stood at ninety-three for eight, dangerously close to the target.

Shilpi, who had bowled really well so far, had only two more overs left. Jasmine asked her to come back. On strike was Chandnisarai's wicketkeeper, Vidhi. She didn't try anything fancy, but managed to get the second ball away for two runs and the next one for a single. Parveen was on strike. Shilpi tore in and bowled a yorker that had Parveen struggling to get out of the way. But somehow, the ball deflected off her bat, missed the stumps and raced to the boundary. Shilpi screamed in rage and frustration.

One hundred for eight. Fourteen runs needed off eighteen balls.

'No more mistakes,' said Jasmine tersely during the team huddle between overs.

Rakhi rose to the occasion and bowled a fairly tight over, giving away only two runs. The Chandnisarai girls were being circumspect too. The rest of their team stood in groups close to the boundary near where Laila was fielding, murmuring nervously.

Twelve needed off twelve balls.

Then, Parveen swung wildly at Shilpi's first delivery. The ball flew off the edge of her bat, over slip and bounced once before crossing the boundary. Eight needed off eleven.

Jasmine walked back with Shilpi to the start of her run-up, arm around her shoulder, talking to her. Shilpi nodded and licked her lips nervously. She waited till Jasmine was back at her position and then ran in for her next ball. Another yorker, which Parveen yet again managed to dig out safely. The ball rolled to mid-on and they ran one.

Seven needed off ten.

Vidhi drove Shilpi's next ball straight down the wicket, where it hit the stumps, sending the bails flying, before deflecting to the mid-on fielder.

'Run, run, run!' Vidhi tore down the wicket. Parveen hesitated, but she ran finally.

Anju was on the ball in a flash. She picked up cleanly and threw it back to Shilpi, who was positioned behind the stumps, in a great position for a sure-shot run-out. But as the bails had already been dislodged, so Shilpi needed to pull a stump out for a run-out to stand. And that gave Vidhi a half second or so extra. She dived for the crease and the umpire ruled not out.

Six needed off nine.

Rattled now, the Chandnisarai girls played out the rest of the over without incident. With six runs needed off the last over, Rakhi came in to bowl.

Parveen smacked at it, driving it hard into the ground and looping up. By the time it landed between cover and mid-off, a run had been taken. Five off five.

Vidhi threw everything at the next ball. It took a thick edge and flew towards gully. Then Jasmine did something

Laila had only seen on TV—she dived full-length, arms outstretched.

There was a stunned silence from the spectators as well as players as she got back to her feet and threw the ball up in the air. Then the spectators erupted and the Rosebud girls swamped their captain.

Chandnisarai's number eleven nervously cross-batted the next delivery to midwicket and tried to take a single where there wasn't one. The match was over. Rosebud had won by the skin of their teeth.

Chapter 17

Rosie Singh, one of Swapna Miss's former India teammates, now a state selector, presented the trophy to Rosebud Academy. It was a modest cup with 'Chandnisarai Girls v Rosebud Academy—Winners' engraved on it, but the Rosebud team were thrilled with it. The crowd cheered gamely when Jasmine went up to receive it, even the Chandnisarai supporters. They had, after all, been treated to a nail-biting game. Jasmine was also adjudged player of the match, and she got a medal for that.

Rosie also gave a short speech, congratulating all the players, and said she had been pleasantly surprised at the quality of cricket on display, considering they had been training for such a short time. 'I will be recommending quite a few of you for the junior state selection camp next season,' she said, 'but before that, you must be waiting for the announcement of the girls selected for the special coaching camp that we are organizing.'

Laila bit her nails nervously as Rosie rustled her papers about.

'From Chandnisarai Girls, Vidhi Kumar, for her incredible wicketkeeping and tail-end batting.'

'Of course,' murmured Jasmine, rocking up and down on the balls of her feet as the subdued Chandnisarai cricketers finally had something to cheer about. The crowd clapped and so did the Rosebud team.

'Parveen Merchant, the most promising young off-spinner I have seen. Rohini Shyam, also a very promising bowler. And Yamini Tripathi, for a cool head, as needed by any middle-order batter.'

She paused. The Rosebud team were still as rocks.

'From Rosebud Academy, Jasmine Barua, extraordinarily skilled batswoman. Shilpi Singhee, who bowled a beautiful line and length. And Laila Malik, whose mature batting display held together her team's innings.'

Laila's ears where ringing as she felt hands thumping her on her back, arms wrapping around her. She was jumping and cheering, for herself, for her friends and, most importantly, for her team.

Samir was quite beside himself with excitement. 'That was the most amazing cricket match I've ever seen that wasn't on TV!'

'Thanks,' said Laila, grinning from ear to ear.

'And congratulations. For the win *and* for getting selected for the camp.'

'Thanks again.'

Murad came bounding up and gave Laila a violent hug. 'You guys were great.'

'We were, weren't we?'

'I'll treat you to ice cream,' he said, even though it was freezing cold. 'Come on. You too, Samir.'

'Can't.' Laila nodded towards her waiting teammates. 'At least not now. I have to go back to school. It's our Parents' Day and we still have to do our history presentation.'

'Oh, right, good luck.'

'Thanks.'

'So, tomorrow, then? For the ice cream?'

'Tomorrow.'

'Okay.' He bounced off again.

'We don't need Sunil Saifi,' said Samir as Laila zipped up her jacket.

'What?'

'I mean, I love cricket, I'll always love it. And I think so do you. No?'

'Yes.' Laila wasn't sure where he was going with this.

'The game is bigger and better than any one person. He can't take it away from us.'

'No,' said Laila quietly. 'You're right. I think I knew that already, but thanks for saying it.'

He nodded. They looked at each other for a second or two.

'I should go...' Laila started to say.

'So, later...' Samir said at the same time.

Laila sped away, a warm, flushed feeling inside her.

It was the last evening before the boarders left for the holidays, so rules were somewhat relaxed. After the parents left, back home or to their hotels for the night, the hostel turned into a disaster zone, with everyone packing and rushing about. Some girls were even leaving that same night. On top of that, there was a general air of celebration because of the match.

The kitchen staff produced a giant cauldron of halwa and rivers of hot chocolate flowed. Most of the day scholars were also hanging out in the dining hall, though it was well past school hours.

'Are you all packed and ready?' Laila asked Prahati and Shalini.

'Yep.' Prahati looked happy. 'I'm leaving tonight. I'll go stay with my parents in the hotel.'

'No hurry for me,' said Shalini with a shrug. 'I'm not leaving till the day after.'

'Where are you going?' Laila asked her when Prahati got up to get more hot chocolate.

'To my aunt's. She's out of town at the moment.'

Laila squeezed her arm. 'So you'll be in town!'

Shalini grinned. 'Looks like it. There are some advantages to not being wanted.'

'Don't say that!'

'Well, it's true. And I've decided that I'm not going to stress over it. For the next few years I'm going to spend most of my life in school anyway. If my parents want to fight over me, it's their problem.'

'You know you can stay at my place if your aunt can't have you,' said Laila.

'I can?'

'Of course! Want to come and stay till your aunt is back?'

Shalini shook her head. 'Jasmine said she'll keep me company.'

'Are you talking about me?' Jasmine, her hair ruffled and sporting a bit of a hot chocolate moustache at the corner of her mouth, plonked down on the chair next to Laila. She looked happier and much more relaxed than they had seen her all semester.

'Yeah. Mean, nasty things, so get out of here,' teased Laila.

'I have deep dark secrets that I can entertain you with.'

'Ooh, tell,' said Shalini. 'I'll trade you one of Laila's secrets: she has a boyfriend!'

'Shalini!' Laila got up, but Shalini was up too. She ran out of the dining hall, once again with Laila at her heels. But this time they were both laughing.

Laila chased her around the quadrangle, and then around the sports shed till Shalini collapsed on the stone bench, clutching her side, still laughing. Jasmine and Prahati had followed them out. Jasmine had some khatta-meetha mixture with her that she shared, though Laila was feeling rather sick from all the halwa.

They sat in silence on the chilly ground, crunching mixture, leaning back against the bench.

'Your history project was great,' said Jasmine after a long silence. 'I didn't know the house had such an interesting history.'

Laila gave her a sideways glance. 'Thanks. Pity we

didn't find any Bollywood celebs.'

Jasmine snorted with laughter.

'It's been one hell of a semester,' said Laila. She looked up at the sky for a few seconds. 'I think I like a boy.'

'Good for you.' Jasmine nudged her with a shoulder. 'My brother did something terrible, but he owned up, so I'm going to try to forgive him.'

'Families are messy,' Shalini put in. 'My parents are splitting up.'

'Ah, shit!' Jasmine said. 'Sorry to hear that.'

'Yeah, thanks.'

'You okay?' asked Prahati.

'No.'

'You will be,' said Laila. She felt it in her bones.

'I know.'

Everyone looked at Prahati, who was studying the sky. She noticed them watching her. 'What?'

'It's your turn,' Laila said, 'to make a deep and meaningful observation about your life.'

Prahati stared blankly. Then she dropped her face in her hands. 'Oh my god! I have no meaning in my life!'

They pelted her with tiny pebbles till she begged for mercy.